Sauntering into Holiness

———

DOUGLAS C. VEST

SOURCE BOOKS   TRABUCO CANYON   CALIFORNIA

Library of Congress Cataloging–in–Publication Data

Vest, Douglas C.
    Sauntering into holiness / Douglas Vest
        p. cm.
    Includes bibliographical references (p.)
    ISBN 0-940147-34-3 (pbk. : alk. paper)
    1. Spiritual life—Christianity. 2. Vest, Douglas C. 3.Deserts–
Religious aspects—Christianity. I. Title.
BV4501.2.V427   1995
242—dc20   95–3738
                                                             CIP

ISBN 0-940147-34-3

Published by:

Source Books
P.O. Box 794
Trabuco Canyon CA 92678

Printed and bound in the USA by KNI Inc., Anaheim CA

dedication
&
acknowledgments

Seeking brevity while describing the contents of this book
in its infancy, I once commented that it is a folksy account
of my twenty–five years of sauntering all over one square
mile of Mojave Desert in California. Sauntering—and on
desert soil—might sound unexciting at first hearing, but the
experience has been entrancing enough to keep me walking
for a quarter century! My hikes, and indeed life's course,
have been enriched by the friendship of Abbot Francis
Benedict OSB, and of Fr. Philip Edwards OSB, who walked from
his profession as a field botanist to monastic duties as
guestmaster of hospitable St. Andrew's Abbey, Valyermo,
CA. I am indebted also to Fr. Maur van Doorslayer OSB, whose
sketches illuminate the text, and to Fr. Werner Morchoven
OSB, whose cover painting invites readers to amble among
fragile desert treasures and into the treasuries of their own
hearts.

contents

1
cotton blowing
in the desert air

The car hastens along the ridge. I am alert for the first glimpse of our destination. The treetops appear, then several low structures among the abundant growth, and I pick out familiar details of the valley. We comment on the cozy setting in the desert below, rather than the backdrop of towering mountains, which have received our murmured tribute for the past twenty miles: winter whiteness, summer shimmering. The mountains are formidable but distant. Soon we shall enter the little valley whose trees, unlike the mountains, are immediately accessible. Our conversation turns to whom and what we might encounter there.

We enter a grove of large cottonwoods which frame the monastery. From the highway during the season of full leafing, the expanse of green is bright against the desert floor. But even in winter's barrenness we look for the trees. In summer, countless leaves move in the slightest breeze, changing in autumn to a brilliant yellow which makes summer's end more acceptable. The gray–white limbs are stripped in winter, when dark clusters of mistletoe are revealed, clinging high, tapping the life–fluid of their hosts. But it is the ebullience of springtime that makes clear why the trees are named cottonwoods. With emerging shiny new leaves of April comes a profusion of fluffy stuff which takes flight at the slightest stirring of the air. One can pick up clumps of the lint–like material from the road. Yet each wind-borne filament is a sail the size of a dandelion parachute, carrying its splinter of a seed.

It is preposterous that such tiny seeds beget the giant trees. Some reach sixty feet. Others are short and thick-waisted from regular pruning. Along a narrow irrigation ditch stands a stocky giant, fully seven feet through its trunk. But the billions of seeds drifting in all directions give birth to only a few trees, so unlikely are sprouting and survival in the desert. Little wonder that such a flurry of cotton must fill the air at fruiting time!

Sitting under one of the trees, I ask myself what issues forth so abundantly in my own life, and conclude that it must be *activity*—my doing, which fills the days as cotton wafting from the trees whitens the air. I seek mentally to defend my excessive bustling, stiffening my back and gaining comfort from knowing that I am like many others in a world much given to whirling industry. But in this setting, part of me is not so defensive. Perhaps my great activity is nothing more than an effort to assure myself that I shall plant something of lasting value in the world—that I should *matter*.

And what can be likened to the blend of circumstances which enable the survival and growth of my efforts—and myself? A true list would be long, and must include: my determination, the support of others, the dependability of natural resources, a legacy of wisdom from the past, and knowing that I live in a universe made possible by a God as profligate in showering gifts upon me as the trees in producing their cotton. The list is qualified by a reluctant recognition of my own perseverance and activity, but the other elements come as special gifts. I survive because of the gifts, and they lift me beyond mere survival to a fuller life otherwise unlikely.

If the cottonwood trees could review their history in California, they might be surprised to be so intimate a part of my reflections. More often they have been valued for their material usefulness, just as I have valued my productivity above my being:

2

...sign of water in the arid lands, fuel in a wooded country, shade where shade is needed most, cottonwoods are mentioned more often than any other vegetation in the literature of early exploration of the open Far West.

Donald C. Peattie, A Natural History of Western Trees

But at this particular monastery, the cottonwoods are important simply in that they exist. Their sturdy presence identifies a restorative oasis in my life. The trees changing vesture, obedient to the rhythm of the seasons, point to the importance of measure and balance, the necessity for quiet periods as well as activity.

I regard my visits to this place as days of recollection, times for collecting myself and my thoughts. No special thought is required once I am there. Stillness embraces me in the shade of a tree, the high desert air hot and dry. There is no agenda, my mind gently wanders, the urge to activity dissolves in the setting, my undriven self becomes reflective. I sense anew why Jesus frequently went away to be refreshed in his most active life.

The cottonwoods are faithful indicators of water in the desert, and water makes life possible. The trees are beneficiaries, and so am I. Relaxed beneath the trees which send roots toward the hidden water, I reach into myself and now and then uncover the quality of life which I overlook when busily jumping between activities. That the water is hidden reminds me that other living water is also present to nourish my spirit. The trees whisper that the nurture can come even when life seems desert-like. And the tiny seeds within the cotton suggest that much growth can come from small beginnings.

3

2
there's more than
lots of sand
in the desert

Desert. For years the word conjured images of desolation, of sand dunes and heat, a place where plants and animals survive on the meager offerings of a land harshly shaped by sun and wind, and the background to strange sounds and scurrying at night. My old unexplored views were limited by lack of personal contact with the desert, and I erred in judging that these omissions yielded a negative sum. I hear assertions about a nearby desert, made more on presupposition or cursory survey than upon experience and patience. Some write off the desert as fearsome, others find it boring, lacking variety, offering little entertainment or comfort. Now I am quick to shout, "Wait! There is so much here!" —even as I forget my own early misgivings.

Because the desert was initially unfamiliar to my senses, I had to search for its subtleties. My appreciation increased as I took up the quest, and I became part of the discovery and the reward. A helpful ally in the exploration was simple curiosity that led me to delve beneath the surface. A less probing companion was periodic reflection. Curiosity highlighted the scenes, and musing let them become part of my outlook and sense of being attracted. I came more and more to see the desert as a true frontier where humanity has left only faint traces of incessant activity.

Centuries ago, the ascetics in their search for God chose to live in such wilderness. Its fabric attracts me now by evoking an internal response deeper than my senses alone afford. I hold within myself what I behold beyond, and thereby extend the encounter to moments when I am elsewhere.

The desert is a fascinating place of hourly changing contrasts and extremes. Colors that are uninteresting when the sun is high, magically change in low light:

> The desert light, producer of the colors, seems almost a physical entity. Its long rays, warm and caressing on an early morning, shift to a hard, hot, flat white glare at noon, then gradually recede to the warm red and pink of the sunset sky; in the waning evening light, cool blue and purple color the distant mountains. Indeed, while much of the coloring of the adjacent desert is in the brown range, the distances are painted in hues of purple.
>
> *Peggy Larson, The Deserts of the Southwest.*

These contrasting colors appear in a variety of settings: flat vegetated areas, eroded cuts in the hills, or smoothly sculpted rock set atilt by the violent movement of the Earth many years ago. The Earth's contour and the sun's light jointly create true kinetic art!

And the desert has other extremes in daytime heat and sharply cool nights. Surface temperatures can rise to 160°F during the day. I cannot keep my hand on this ground, yet plants and trees have evolved to tolerate the baking. Dryness cannot be taken for granted, for sudden rain and flash–floods rushing down flat, dry washes, alter the course of roads on which travelers rely. There are but few conduits cut by regular rainfall, so the infrequent torrents spread violently and can sweep away cars.

Personal safety is a serious business here. A water bottle, walking stick, and a companion are advisable when hiking far afield. Short, individual walks are more relaxed, when snakes are hibernating rather than in the shadow of the next bush. Desert life itself is vulnerable to intrusion, and so I tread lightly around its creatures.

John Steinbeck was not enthusiastic about desert in *The Grapes of Wrath:*
And [Route] 66 goes on over the terrible desert, where the distance shimmers and the black cinder mountains hang unbearably in the distance.
The long barren stretch was an obstacle to the migrants. In contrast, I experience the now familiar desert near my home as a place of rest. Its apartness lets me get away from what is routine and burdensome in my daily life. The scarcity of its plants is a relief from an overload of what the crowded city offers. Wide daily shifts in temperature provide stimulus instead of lethargy in a climate of slight seasonal changes. Contrasts in color and vegetation suggest that difference can be valued in other areas of life. Clarity of the air lets me see distant details. The short periods of peak colors among the blossoms remind me to enjoy beauty when it is offered.

My visits to the desert have taken on a monthly pattern: time intervals which recall the wide spacing of perennial plants on the desert floor. I have come to realize that this scattered pattern does not result from a shortage of seeds, but is a self-regulating way of survival. Wide-spreading, shallow roots take in the water from brief showers so effectively that seeds at the soil's surface do not have access to moisture which would allow them to germinate. What I had taken to be an inability of potential plants to sprout and grow, is in fact a protection of the plants already there. A further regulation is found within some seeds themselves: natural inhibitors which prevent sprouting until substantial rain has leached out the delaying chemical. Still later I recognize that other types of plants, which appear leafless much of the year, are not dead, but dormant. The desert is remarkably self-regulating—and it sets forth a good example of living with limitations. I trust that it might awaken what goes into hiding within myself.

3
beauty to a fault

Our home is near the edge of a spreading urban area, nestled in the rusticity of a small canyon. The silence which blesses us is seldom broken by noise from a busy traffic artery four blocks downhill. The home is a private place by its very setting. Access to our canyon is by a single-lane curved driveway, into which a large boulder protrudes on one side, and a drop of ten or so feet looms on the other—sufficient test for alertness whether driving out or in.

When leaving home for a day that is tightly planned, I gird myself mentally to deal both with competitive traffic and my own busyness. In contrast, a journey's start is quite different for a quiet day in the desert. These occasions begin in a far more relaxed way. On this particular day, I ease into the morning, telling myself in loose rhyme that my mental focus will depend upon the physical locus, location gently guiding the hours I have to spend in another friendly setting. There is no need to rush along the highway that crosses the mountains. Travel through the scenery of unbuilt countryside is part of the day's pleasure.

My destination is not many miles distant as birds would travel but, in a measure typical of the city, an hour and one quarter from home by car. The time passes easily, rewarding me with sights of ever-new familiar objects and panoramic views *en route*, then closing with thankfulness for a safe journey and anticipation of whatever will be experienced during my stay.

The monastery to which I drive frequently is situated within a small valley formed by low foothills that reach toward mountain peaks about ten miles away. The unadorned buildings are inviting in their simplicity. Those sturdy cottonwood trees are in full green canopy today. Low structures stand among them, some mainly of white-painted wood, and others of gray concrete blocks. I know that the nearby cottonwoods thrive where there is a steady supply of water, and judge that an ample underground supply lies below the dry surface.

Bright evidence of water's nurturing power lies on either side of my parking place: a wide, grassy lawn sloping downward from an old stone ranch house and another area, a stone's throw downhill, where cattle sometimes graze behind a white board fence. The greenness is at first startling against the brown background of the hillside on this warm spring day. A sizeable shaded pond within a dimple of the Earth near the two grassy areas, also owes its replenishment to a large pump throbbing steadily, two miles from the buildings and several nearby sprinklers which have been active since before my arrival.

The greenery of the trees and lawns validates the place as an oasis intentionally maintained between a creek bed and two layers of foothill ridges above. What was once Hidden Springs Ranch is now Saint Andrew's Abbey, the home of a monastic community nurtured both by the water and by community prayers offered several times daily. A witty person might exclaim, "A wise practice, those prayers!" For about a half mile towards the mountains is massive evidence of nature's fragility—indeed of the Earth's structure itself. A dramatic depression named the Devil's Punch Bowl is located there, offspring of a brief but passionate meeting of the San Jacinto and San Andreas Earth Faults, many years ago.

'Earthquake' evokes many negative feelings and thoughts: 'everything out of control...thrust upon us without warning...selectively damaging... Only thirty seconds? It seemed to last forever!' Those who have recently experienced a vigorous shaking of the Earth are little interested in technical explanations: whether the land's drunken movement results from the release of forces long stored in the distorted skin of a cooling and shriveling Earth, from the slippage of Earth plates, or for other reasons—even 'earthquake weather,' as some people speculate! Nor are residents near a temblor's epicenter consoled by suggestions that the recent activity of faults in southern California has not occurred directly along the San Andreas line, but along its younger offshoots.

Who more readily than the monks of St. Andrew's can be forgiven for muttering in nervous humor, 'San Andreas, forgive us our faults?' Joining the chorus, I remark aside to the Earth, 'And by the way, thanks for the attractive scenery you have created.' Displacement of earth along the San Andreas Rift has not only shaped the Devil's Punch Bowl, now encircled by a convenient mile-long hiking trail, but it also accounts for a string of scenic views along a 700–mile north–south line in California. Several locations exhibit markedly contrasting colors where the Rift has broken through rock. Other sections are now flat washes. The Rift reaches its highest point in the notch of a mountain–top overlooking the Abbey.

At several locations along the San Andreas line, sharp cliffs rise out of flat, expansive valleys in natural disruptions of the Earth's surface. Viewed from the air, the Fault's width is seen to vary from a scant hundred yards to perhaps a mile. There is much variety and beauty in the surface display, born of violent shaking! I reckon that a totally smooth Earth, never subjected to surface readjustments wrought by cooling and shrinking, would offer very few scenic wonders!

Another dramatic north–south line has been incised by human enterprise down the center of the state: a section of the California Aqueduct that carries water 445 miles from the Sacramento Delta to Lake Perris, southeast of Los Angeles, via an open channel more than one hundred feet wide. The course of this conduit is well-chosen for its directness, but it lies precariously (it would seem) near the San Andreas Rift, and even to cross the Fault in several places. I wonder critically why much of the channel was constructed so close to a notorious line of trouble, then confront an obvious possible reason: the viaduct's route had been already prepared, in large measure, by seismic forces!

But another question arises: why are long stretches of the channel open to the dry desert air, so eager to evaporate the water? Again it is because the Earth's fault lies there. The Aqueduct cannot be enclosed by concrete or mountain soil, but must be accessible for quick repair in case the Earth's crust adjuster should again misbehave. So, along a path dictated by the shifting Earth's surface, billions of gallons of water flow daily, sharing its bounty along the way.

Life–giving water flows along the Earth's cleft. I realize, though I would not choose it so, that my own periods of disruption have allowed God's deeper entrance into my life. It does not matter at such times whether that is true because I have admitted the God I have held 'out there,' or because I recognize afresh the God who has been nearby all the while. I do sense that wholeness can start to build from the new openness. I like to think that such wholeness also indicates a new openness to holiness.

Must I wait until hard times are inflicted upon me before I can let myself be open to the divine? I know that the answer is no, and I reflect on the health–giving nature of contact with other Christians, with individual or group spiritual guidance, through childlike prayer, and my own honest awareness of what is happening in my life. I do not need to deny either the painful or the pleasant. Admitting what is actual can be the start of new health...wholeness...holiness.

Normally Pallett Creek is a narrow border on the north side of the Abbey grounds. In flood times it widens to almost a hundred feet, and carries an unruly flow equal to that which the Aqueduct regularly delivers. More usually the stream is indolent and elusive. One day I traced a noisy little brook coursing through the spread–out stones, easily stepping across the stream several times for drier footing on the opposite side. But less than a hundred yards from my entrance point, the flow slackened—then disappeared! What had happened to the flowing water? Little matter: water had reached this point and was coming from farther up the wide course of rocks, so there must be more water ahead! Sure enough, a damp spot appeared a hundred yards ahead, then visible water, and again a lively flow. Investigation well downstream showed that there was nothing unique about my point of entry to the stream, for a similar hide-and-seek behavior was acted out below as well.

I surmise how the disappearing trick is carried out: The flow disappears when it finds and sinks into a sandy bed, flows downhill out of sight in the porous layer, and is later diverted upward into full view upon encountering an impervious layer of rock.

So much for a technical explanation! Is there something personally helpful I can learn from the rich image of the now-you-see-me-now-you-don't creek? My first reaction is that a more anxious person might focus on malevolent forces loose in the world. I do not dismiss the subject with defensive humor, nor by citing Sophocles' remark more than two millennia ago: "To him who is in fear, everything rustles."

I have been favored by a rich life marked by traumas and periods of recovery, so my response to the creek's presence-absence lies in a more positive direction. In several stages of life, I have felt Jesus as a dear friend walking with his arm about my shoulder. But there have been other times when

I have forgotten that presence. Those moments have felt much like abandonment. In future I shall try to recall the creek. My periodic inability to perceive God's presence does not mean that the divine support is not at work in both my painful and joyful moments, waiting to surface in my awareness somewhat later, as little Pallett Creek does in its journey to join Big Rock Creek.

I know these things when I take time to reflect, but will my impatience demand some early sign that the Lord really is aware in my troubled moments? This late spring day, I look from the almost dry creek bed to mountain peaks a few miles away. Their moderate snow cover promises relief from the drought which has visited California for the past several years. The creek runs full when thaw time reaches the heights, but will there be more underground water for the hidden springs next year? Hardly that soon, one of the resident monks informs me. Snow now visible in the mountains' shaded depressions will not find its way into the underground reservoirs until the third year. Whether that means three full years or a calendar year with bits of two other years, I do not enquire. But at least I know that patience will be required.

14

4
birds at work
and play

I was simply walking, generally aware of my geographical bearings, but of little else. My mood was of a pervasive lostness, caught in a tangle of emotions—mainly feeling very sorry for myself after the death of my wife Alice, and not ready to be lifted out of the gloom. I had chosen to be alone and thus free of others' agenda. The course was safe to tread without concern about footing: smooth road surface, desert terrain sloping gently from the road, very little automobile traffic.

The morning's stillness was consoling, its muteness contrasting with a slight sound that arose from the darting movement of a covey of quail feeding on the downhill slope nearby. One bird was motionless, apart on a rock about

eighteen inches high, not eating, but serving as a sentinel for a dozen others. The solitary one moved its head radar-like from side to side, sounding a periodic musical tch-tch-tch while surveying the area where its companions fed.

After watching for ten or fifteen minutes, I approached quietly, curious to learn what would happen when the birds sensed my closing presence. Though intently watching them, I was startled by the sudden whirring sound of their simultaneous takeoff into flight. All but the sentinel flew away to an area some fifty or sixty feet from their initial feeding spot, and settled among the low dry plants of a small raised area. Only after the covey had relocated and resumed their foraging for seeds, did the sentry join the others and take up a new observation position, this time not voicing its reassuring sound, but obviously keeping watch.

Aware that I was intruding upon their ease, I withdrew very slowly lest I again disturb the feeding birds. My easy movement was graciously paralleled by a gentle current within: before I had returned to my room in the retreat house, I felt some assurance that a Lord who provides good shepherds (and even guard-birds!) had not abandoned me in the discomfort of my bereavement.

Deep acceptance of this dependable presence would require the passage of some months before I could truly accept it, but the simple encounter which 'just happened' would prove to be a very important event in my life. In a lighter vein, my curiosity still inclines me to observe the movements and manners of quail wherever they reveal themselves in other desert settings. I give thanks for their part in my psychic healing, and because they are gentle creatures with whom I can play hide-and-seek.

On subsequent walks, I relearn what I had experienced as a child in another part of the country: that quail are quicker to react to my presence than I to theirs! Sometimes they scamper into the distance, but usually they fly away low in the brush with a startling swish. Invariably I feel a slight rush of adrenaline that readies me to deal with an unforeseen threat quite out of proportion to what has swooped before me. Surprised again and again by the gentle birds, and quickened by the adrenaline, I become aware of being alive and vital—and that I am thankful. I respond with a milder greeting than my quickened pulse urges, calling out to them in some affectionate way.

Because the quail are so quick on their feet, and keep a good distance from perceived danger, it is difficult for me to characterize their colors and markings. A California quail is a generous handful in size and adorned with several colors and distinctive markings. *Audubon's Field Guide* provides details:

> Colorfully and intricately patterned. Creamy forehead and black throat. Crown and throat edged in white. Grayish-blue breast and softly mottled nape; unstreaked brown back and creamy belly scaled with brown markings. Creamy diagonal streaking. Female less boldly marked than male...
> *Audubon Society Field Guide, Western Region.*

Altogether a fascinating bit of walking artwork! Most noticeable is a bouncing plume that extends forward over the topknot, more suggestive of a short fishing pole than bangs of hair over a forehead. Out front is a flat plumage of feathers more than a quarter inch across and an inch long, terminating its threadlike holder. The bobbing seems not a major distraction, for the birds rapidly peck first this way, then that, plumes keeping time with their darting footwork.

In my grief, my heart was touched to hear that a quail has but one mate, and that several families merge to form a covey. I learn too that they do not beget families in years of short food supply. Sometimes when I observe their cohesive groupings, searching for tiny seeds, I catch the image of an extended family that is both industrious and responsible. As the sentinel quail demonstrated, their concern for each other goes beyond the wisdom of safety in numbers. The quails offer me several matters to ponder concerning human relationships—and they respectfully maintain silence while I ponder.

Not so silent is a much larger raven which noisily sounds a coarse croak from its lazy flight, from its perch on a leafless tree, or from most anywhere whence it can call for attention: "See what I am about to do...and do again and again!" Reacting to the sound, I find myself doubting whether several large black birds are playing like daredevil children in the sky! Yes, they are riding an aerial surf along a ridge, no more than two hundred yards from where I stand. They return in elliptical flight to approach the end of the ridge at my right, move their wings vigorously for a bit, and then glide for a hundred yards or more along a thermal updraft which continuously flows up the sunlit side of the ridge. The birds coast, perhaps thirty feet above the Earth. Apparently the air moves not only upward but also to the left of my position, for the ravens glide in that direction, needing to flap their wings only occasionally to maintain a critical elevation.

But do ravens actually roll in flight? They seem to do complete sidewise rotations, a feat I had ascribed only to power-driven aircraft! Whether or not my eyes inform me well, the birds are quite evidently enjoying the play, for again and again they fly back to the low edge of the ridge to make yet another cavorting flight. They provide a good antidote to my taking myself too seriously at times, flying playfully when the conditions are right, and doing something else between times.

I can relate to the quails' valuing family life, and to the playful ravens who know how to enjoy life as individuals, but of all the desert birds, the red-tailed hawk comes closest to exposing my envy. They soar high in the sky, and from the heights they can see 'the big picture'—so I fancy. A hawk seems to locate an object which attracts, and moves directly to it. My inclination to efficiency admires the ability to focus and prioritize!

The hawk's visual acuity is astounding, but it is its high soaring which most attracts me. I need to remember, however, that soaring does not come immediately—for hawks or for myself. While on a solitary walk, I was privileged to witness the movement of a red–tailed hawk from its perch on a cottonwood limb to the heights above. Its first effort was a vigorous flapping of wings, from the tree to an elevation of perhaps fifty feet. Then it shifted to what I judged to be a flight–test phase: gliding for half or more of a large circular path, then necessarily flapping its wings as it continued to rise. Somewhat higher, it was able to glide effortlessly, and thereafter it soared and circled and soared. I have no doubt that the hawk was enjoying itself famously!

The bird's evident enjoyment still fascinates me. I am convinced that it did not go aloft in search of prey that might be moving on the ground, but that the soaring was more lighthearted than the needs of survival. I wonder what led the hawk to push off from a limb of the tree. Was the determining stimulus a stirring of the wind or a stirring within? Was the hawk perhaps following a pleasant memory of another flight? If that was true, the memory was sufficiently vivid to sustain the effort of clumsy preliminaries before reaching the heights where other forces could take over.

5
sauntering

I like to walk! Often I find myself in motion without having thought much about beginning to move. When I resist the prospect, likely it is because I have already found comfort in not doing much of anything, perhaps feeling close to a state of simply *being* and not wanting to interfere with that rare sensation. More usually, an urge to walk comes because I seek a refreshing change from what I have been doing.

Several days ago I reckoned that the first few steps of a walk remind me of an appetite for food. When hungry I want to change whatever else has been taking place—ceasing work and taking food, perhaps. With a hearty appetite, the first few mouthfuls of almost any palatable food are most gratifying. So it is that I welcome a walk after prolonged inactivity.

But the rewards of leisurely walking cannot be explained solely by the preceding deprivation. Movement reminds me that my body feels good in motion, when its many members act in concert and bring a sense of wholeness. Open, wide-ranging thought also contributes to the renewal, for I prefer to walk when not responding to a necessity that has been thrust upon me.

A brisk walk might serve the practical purpose of clearing my busy head, and bring the feeling that I have a number of options about what next direction to let my whole body move. At other times a thinly veiled curiosity leads me to step out, and movement delivers me to explore what might have aroused the search. No doubt there are moments when walking reassures me that I am still able to get around in a sprightly manner, for my personality is likely shaped by a view of myself as active. The movement is a simple liturgy of being. Since it is being in the present, I do not borrow trouble about the future.

I especially treasure morning walks when nature's liveliness is becoming evident after the hours of darkness. If I were more an owl than a lark (as those slow to waken are sometimes distinguished from the quick risers) I would more probably bestir myself in afternoons or evenings. But curiosity nurtures a preference for mornings—for instance, what are the birds and bunnies doing?—And I detect a gentle, inner urge to go beyond myself and transcend my oneness.

The best response I can make to that invitation is *motion*. Walking transports me both to wander and to wonder, wonder as both noun and verb: to experience awe and to ponder it. As the owls are retiring and the larks arising, I feel part of the awakening world and experience a union with nature which I value.

Thoreau's 1862 essay *Walking* reveals him to have been a man almost rabid on the subject (and practice): four hours or more per day, he professed. Indeed his proclivity for ambulation extended to criticism of his neighbors

> who confine themselves to shops and offices the whole day for weeks and months, ay, and years together. I know not what manner of stuff they are of—sitting there now at three o'clock in the afternoon as if it were three o'clock in the morning...I wonder about this time, or say between four and five o'clock in the afternoon, too late for the morning papers and too early for the evening ones, there is not a general explosion heard up and down the street, scattering a legion of antiquated and house-bred notions and whims to the four winds for an airing.

Thoreau further avowed that he had met 'but one or two persons in the course of my life who understand the art of Walking.'

My focus is not outward, to assess others. I would neither chide nor pity anyone who resists frequent walking. Quite the contrary, I give thanks that I am able to walk—as grateful for mobility as for an appetite! But unlike Thoreau, I do not believe that one earns winged shoes by intentionally combining thoughtful reflection with movement:

> ...you must walk like a camel, which is said to be the only beast which ruminates when walking.

However, reflection does happen with dependable regularity as images and thoughts ease into my consciousness during solitary walks. I discover a quiet introspection, a comforting relief from extravert tendencies and the inclination to stay busy as a validation of my existence.

No doubt a number of people have learned that walking provides a good setting for sorting potential responses to questions pressing into personal awareness. My interest is not so practical or intentional, but 'walking for walking's sake' as artist Paul Klee has written. My mood is generally one of recreation or taking it easy, so I merely begin to walk in a direction which seems momentarily attractive. With such a gentle start I do not resist departing from a much-traveled way to investigate a new region. So a sense of freedom ensues. Nor would I consider it an intrusion to stop and admire an object or scene, or to pause to make a brief written note for later reflection. Objects are not there in some general way as mere elements of an environment, but as specifics present to be admired. What draws me to a particular object? It could be curiosity, but that is not usual. Perhaps I sense that a gift is there, special to the occasion.

If I change course impulsively, the impulses are no more forceful than nudges. Altogether, I enjoy the flow of a mild, buoyant current, and do not need long pauses for rest along the way. Indeed when the pauses become prolonged, they often signal the end of the relaxed walk, and I return to my home at a brisk gait. That invigoration, too, is well received.

Thoreau probably would have called it sauntering:

> I have met with but one or two persons in the course of my life who understood the art of Walking...who had a genius, so to speak, for *sauntering:* which word is beautifully derived from 'idle people who roved about the country in the Middle Ages, and asked charity, under pretence of going *a la Sainte Terre,* to the Holy Land, till the children exclaimed 'There goes a Sainte–Terrer,' a Saunterer—a Holy–Lander... Some, however, would derive the word from *sans terre,* without land or a home, which therefore, in the good sense, will mean having no particular home, but equally at home everywhere. For this is the secret of successful sauntering.

Sauntering, or by whatever name carefree walking may be called, has one advantage which runs counter to my achieving, active spirit: the increased likelihood that I can be overtaken! Fortunately, the frequent overtakers are not malevolent characters, but discrete inner discoveries ushered inward by the senses—the sight of a tiny flower hugging the dry earth, the call of a distant bird, or the sharp odor of a stand of creosote bushes. I fantasize that an array of thoughts and feelings have hovered near my consciousness for some days or weeks until I become relaxed and ready to be hospitable: rather like a pond beneath their migration path inviting mallard ducks to cease their flight.

The gentle insights which overtake my sauntering self are seldom dramatic, but I treasure these gifts enough to muse about them in an intentional way. One day as I was completing a hike on the Abbey grounds, I noted a large rock alongside the road, perhaps pushed aside when the roadway to the monastic cemetery had been cleared several years earlier. The rock is about four feet high, five feet long and two thick. In some defiance of maximum stability, the rock sits on an edge, rather than a more expansive side. I project that its posture is the product of an artistic eye and the dexterity of a bulldozer operator. In any case, someone cared enough to leave a legacy alongside the road. The rock could have been pushed aside years ago, but I imagine that the driver responded to a challenge and that a particular curve in the road was thereafter made different from the flat desert all around it.

Of course, the rock could have been left upended for no particular reason, with no intention to leave an artistic marker. I abandoned that thought as I continued my walk on a sandy path around the nearby pond, where the absence of footprints argued that another artistic effort had been accomplished very recently. About that circuit I later wrote in my journal:

The sandy path alongside the ranch house end of the duck pond has been neatly raked, and many parallel lines remain from the rake's passage. The stone retaining wall beside the path provides a shaded place at one end where I sat briefly. On much of the rest of the wall, unbound bundles of cottonwood twigs have been tidily placed. The twigs rest in alignment on the wall in a number of small piles, not a tangled stack in a corner. It is as if each twig represents a life issue, and the tangled questions of my life have been separated so that each may be handled—taken in hand and held, and turned and admired, and placed elsewhere—and maybe even discarded. Now they are simply on the wall, and there are seven stacks, each of a size that could be held within the grasp of two hands.

As I review these journal notes about an easy stroll that led me past a large rock and some bundled twigs, I recall words penned in the seventeenth century by Thomas Traherne, a writer who has touched my heart in several of his writings:

> To walk abroad is, not with Eys, But thoughts…And evry thing that I did see Did with me talk.

Over the years, I have come more and more to view Traherne's writings to be not inept verse, as I once judged, but childlike in a way that opens me to wonder. As I walk with friends who are visiting one of my favorite haunts for their first time, I suspect that some of them have bypassed childhood and now yearn for a way to enjoy simple pleasures, yet are quite uncertain about how to go about the search. In them I detect a mild confusion which considers that some sorts of imaginings are adult, and others immature. Removing that artificial barrier does wonders in opening my heart and bidding all of me to wonder about what I encounter. I ponder whether this is a preparation for entering the Kingdom of God about which Jesus spoke so often!

Another sentiment expressed about Traherne invites me to hurdle some of my preconceptions and begin to explore creation in a relaxed, sauntering way:

> In Traherne we see how aesthetic delight, religious awe and wonder, scientific curiosity and investigation, all lie very close to one another.
> A. M. Allchin, 'Commentary on Heaven' in Fairacres Chronicle, Spring 1990.

These words describe my experience so well that I wish I had expressed them. In my walks, however, I recognize that I have been disarmed by wonder, led into exploration by a free-floating curiosity, given a new appreciation for beauty, and enriched by my meditative treasuring of what has been encountered—perhaps recovering part of a lost childhood as well!

6
busy ant traffic

My initial inclination was to forgo a leisurely walk in favor of a brisk two–mile hike to a roadway turnaround near the end of the Abbey property. That plan soon changed. The early morning air had been refreshingly cool beneath the large cottonwood trees, but now a bright sun was announcing the buildup of August heat along the blacktop roadway. Ordinarily the hike I envisioned was not daunting, but the heat soon to come would be unwelcome along the unshaded course. I might be wiser, I reckoned *en route,* to abandon the mild urge for heroics and simply respond to whatever diversion seemed appropriate somewhere uproad.

The choice between an energetic or leisurely walk was resolved a scant half–mile from my start, soon after an ant crossed my path. The encounter with the tiny insect began just as I seated myself on a bench which memory reminded me was located beneath a clump of leafy trees. I didn't recognize the ant as a long–term acquaintance. But like many other ants I had met over the years, this one struggled along with a sizeable burden, passing just a few inches from my shoes. Now aware that my destination had likely changed, I resolved to learn where the ant might be heading. Its journey would be slow by my standards, but rapid by ant criteria, despite the relatively irregular terrain.

Perhaps I should have rejoiced in being not so exertive as the ant this hot day! What first impressed me was the immensity of the ant's burden relative to its size: a tan–

colored tuft of something, perhaps the seed end of a stalk of grass. The object was held out in front, a miniature version of a husky Scotsman plodding forward to toss a pine–log caber in Highland Games. "Much stem, little seed for food," I mused.

By shifting my position after it passed the end of the bench, I was able to observe that the ant's course was proportionately shorter than the four miles I had contemplated for myself. Coarse–packed sand allows comfortable walking in human shoes, but some particles were equivalent to boulder-size obstacles for the insect. Forward the ant went, more darting than plodding, its strong mandibles holding the load up and forward, and six legs feeling the way along the moonscape surface it was traversing. After about ten minutes, the ant came to three small openings in a well–packed surface of the earth: three holes in a foot–long alignment on the sand. The two outward orifices were about three–fourths of an inch diameter, and the central one, double that width. The tiny creature lurched beyond the midpoint of the alignment, and went directly to the more distant right-hand hole. It paused there with load still firmly grasped, while several outbound ants passed close by. Then it did an about-face, moved toward the large central opening, and entered without further hesitation.

So much for the short acquaintance! Ants continued to exit from the opening—but how was I to know when or if the carrier might reappear during my stay? I fancied that it had received some message or a reward beneath the surface of the earth. What happened to the burden? How was the seed tuft transported and stored in the totally dark recess underground? Indeed, what was the nature of the interior of the ant colony: how deep was the storehouse, and of what configuration—and what design kept the structure's dome from collapsing?

I was limited, of course, to investigating the brightly lighted surface, but was still curious, and visually retraced my new friend's former course. Two ants came into sight, jointly carrying a large near-circular, flat seed, one ant pulling and the other pushing, it seemed. The seed appeared to be compact and dense, and I resisted the temptation to touch the object whose bulk I judged equivalent to my struggling with a full barrel of material. Although slower than the original transporter, this pair followed the same curved course the lone carrier had chosen. There must be truth in the reports that ants lay down an odor trail, I reckoned, for this active pair did not hesitate in moving along a zigzag path until they reached the central opening. A brief moment of indecision ensued, then further movement to the right-hand hole. One of the ants released its hold on the seed and entered that port, passing several exiting ants that paused near the lone guard of the seed, as if to send some greeting or transmit a practical advisory.

After waiting for some twenty or thirty seconds, the husky one reversed course and carried the seed unassisted to the largest opening, and let the burden rest on the ground. Several ants appeared from below and approached the scene with antennae waving vigorously. Then followed a delay of about five minutes while a number of ants emerged, carrying large grains of sand. They were, I presumed, clearing a path and perhaps a storage place for the oversize treasured find— perhaps the first such prize of the day. The ensuing activity was frenzied, though evidently well engineered, for the removed particles were carried well away from the opening: a foot or more, in what I thought might be the beginning of a large circle of the sort I have often seen on the desert floor. Its way well prepared, the lone trucker carried the seed and disappeared into the opening.

The busyness in clearing the food cache and its opening anticipated a bonanza of food, for within several minutes other seeds were moving down the miniature pathway a dozen or more feet distant. A major project was under way, and the transporters were working effectively in pairs.

I sauntered back to my room without posing for myself the further adventure of backtracking the ant trail to locate the source of the precious seeds. I reasoned at the time that the morning had already provided a rich experience of probing beyond myself. Anyhow, I can always locate scores of other ants near other anthills during all but the coldest months. Or it could have been that one of God's busiest creatures had freed me of the urge for activity on a day which became hot enough as to be downright unfriendly.

The story was a good one to relate next day at a workshop I was co–leading at the Abbey. Though the telling was about the ants, I later realized that the insects provided much data about myself. I learned anew that I am taught well by nature's tiny creatures. Though dramatic events teach dramatically, they can also traumatize. I seek out the gentle, and avoid the powerful.

I was curious about the underground structure of the ants' home, giving less thought at the time to my own structures about life in general or the spiritual life in particular. I too am a very busy person, goal–oriented, and inclined to go alone as the two principal ant actors had been. These thoughts came later, as I reaffirmed the importance of reflecting on the gift of life and not merely relating its adventures to others. As true as Søren Kierkegaard's comment that the Bible was written for me and about me, so are the offerings of creation. Insights can be grasped. God makes that possible; I help them to burst forth.

7
night watch

Sometimes when at my home near Los Angeles, I fancy myself elsewhere as a lone camper in a desert region. In imagination, I walk into an enveloping darkness, leaving behind the faint glow of the few embers remaining from my supper's fire. Except for the overhead light spread as countless sparks across the heavens, my course lies in total darkness. There are no household lights to illumine my course, not even a distant city's aura reflected from the undersides of clouds hovering over the horizon. The major source of brightness is a half–moon, too radiant to be gazed at fixedly through clean air. The stars are crisply bright; some in groupings that have borne imaginative names over the centuries: the Water Bearer, Big Bear, and Pegasus the winged horse.

I recollect these sights because I have seen them often through desert air at the monastery. During evening walks there, several light standards which offer safety for visitors dull my view of the sky, but a few hundred yards from the buildings, the heaven's lights return. Stars are so numerous that I scan the dome overhead and around the horizon, and can only mutter in astonishment. I behold many universes from Earth, the tiny satellite of a star we know as Sun!

Depending upon both month and hour, the moon is the most obvious of the luminaries. In daylight, it often can be easily located overhead. On some evenings when the moon is hidden at sunset, it glides visible in the east with a brightness that casts long shadows westward. As a special treat in late September, the relative positions of Earth and this glowing satellite combine their brightness for several consecutive nights. No wonder this gift of added illumination has been valued for centuries as Harvest Moon, rising close upon the sun's setting and prolonging the period of working light for grain harvest before the advent of inclement weather. The extra light is provided just when needed! So it seems that much needed support comes to me when two things combine: I let my needs be known in prayer or sharing, and I am receptive.

But the wonders of the sky extend far beyond bigness and brightness. The most startling view of the moon I have seen in the desert setting was simply a bright upper cusp, half of a crescent moon—no more than an upturned sliver showing above a nearby hilltop because the moon was well underlighted by the sun already set. Like a shark's fin much out of place, the curved blade of light appeared above a nearby high point on the Earth's surface. I was mildly perturbed that things were not exactly as I thought they should be!

The clarity of desert air by day or night reveals spectacular views of this nearest celestial object. One quarter of a million miles distant, the moon is next door, compared with the other objects in the background, before which the moon moves as the night hours progress. The coming of night reminds me that the wondrous Moon is but one of a countless host overhead. The evening sky seems carpeted with tiny lights as profusely as a meadow filled with daisies or buttercups or bluebells. The heavens seem close, and teem with so many bright points that it looks white along the wide band of the Milky Way. I am reminded that the surface lights of my home city prevent seeing beyond the thin layer of air surrounding the Earth. Human creations obscure the natural! I am part of the cloudiness.

34

In the desert the intensity of lunar light discourages nighttime use of binoculars, except for momentary glances. But the glasses help to locate fainter objects. At first I was surprised to find that they enlarged very few of the heavenly lights. Those few that can be seen enlarged are the planets. Venus, misnamed the Evening Star, shows phases of full or partial illumination much as the Moon does. Viewed through high-powered glasses, Saturn might reveal its rings, and Jupiter its giant red spot. In contrast, the stars do not reveal such details, for they appear no larger in the glasses than the unaided eye judges them to be.

A telescope does not enlarge much that is seen in the heavens either. However, more objects are seen—so many more! Within the constellation of Taurus, Pleiades is perceived as a cluster of stars, of which the unassisted eye can make out six, notwithstanding their popular nickname: The Seven Sisters of Atlas. With increasingly great magnification, I could see the much larger company of more than two thousand. Once again I am reminded that the instruments do not enlarge the objects, but reveal a greater number of them. Nor do my projects of prayer or study or meditation bring the already-present God any closer; but I become aware of the richness of that presence as I prepare the way for my awareness.

Can it be that the stars which I behold during a night walk, are really at an infinite distance from where I stand? Yes, it is so. Printed facts tell me that such and such a star is so many light–years distant (a number which I can turn over and over in my mind, and even cite as if I actually comprehend), but the object remains at virtually infinite distance. So it is with life's mysteries, and so it is in human efforts to change the dimensions of God. I sometimes want God to be responsive to my wishes or even whims—God on call, brought sensibly closer and even compliant! I seem not yet ready to accept God's presence without validating that presence with my senses.

The telescope reveals many more stars than I can imagine as I walk in the night. Back over a shoulder lies Ursa Major, whose better known part is the Big Dipper, a configuration of but six (or is it seven) visible stars. The Dipper's pouring lip points to Polaris, the North Star which has been long the companion of those who travel by land or sea in the northern hemisphere. My eyes follow the line of the Pointers and locate the navigator's friend, near enough to the horizon that it does not roam the sky as the earth rotates in the night. I can distinguish the relatively dim Pole Star because the Pointers inform my search. I reflect that there are many pointers of different sorts which might be helpful in my spiritual search, and I wonder if I am availing myself of these aids.

Polaris has been party to many explorations in the northern hemisphere. But not all discoveries are of those celebrated voyages of earlier times! There are explorations which can attract the patient observer in practical and playful ways. In the middle of the Dipper's handle is a double star. The Bedouins once called the paler star The Faint One, and the other The Veil, or Cloak. I first heard the pair referred to as The Test, for the two offer a simple way to assess vision. The faint light of Alcor shows alongside the dominant Mizar, but where on the clock face can it be seen, if at all? With my eyeglasses I can answer the question. Without them, I cannot. My visual acuity has obviously diminished since boyhood! I wonder whether my sense of wonder has also suffered.

An exciting year in early adolescence brought me an awareness of both the telescope and the microscope. With youthful intensity, I explored tiny things close up, and enormous objects at unimaginable distances. There seemed no limit to what I could probe, smaller and smaller in one case, and ever larger in the other—if I just had access to the instruments! Even so, a number of years passed before I could acknowledge that these new visions were possible because assisting devices had been made available by persons unknown to me. In all of my excitement, I was reluctant to admit that I was so recently thrilled by what others had enjoyed for centuries.

Still more time was needed before I realized that the new sights changed my concept of creation, not only quantitatively according to size, but also qualitatively in the manner of how I interpreted those sights. A drop of murky water below the microscope lens revealed fascinating living things, each complete with its life organs.

With telescope in hand, I wondered time and again why there was a large black spot in the heavens. One explanatory theory, reaching my ears much later, is that the nothingness results from a dying star whose collapse attracts all matter from an enormous surrounding expanse, drawing it into a tininess difficult for the mind to conceive. The vicinity of the star's death scene is so altered that nothing, not even light, can escape. Therefore, this particular theory argues, conditions within this whirlpool of space and time are such that an observer outside could not relate understandable times with what takes place within, so communication would not be possible.

At first fearful that I cannot break through to God, I take comfort in the likelihood that One who created the wonders I probe can also reach out to me in a love which touches my very center.

8
a burning bush

It all began with a quick glance to my left, outward viewing and inward searching. At times I am conscious that my eyes tend to dart when I would have them behave otherwise. I once heard that blue eyes, especially light blue, are inclined to do so. Now I tell myself that my eyes wander because they are blue.

No doubt I glance here and there hundreds of times each day, yet instants thereafter release most of what I have just glimpsed. I have wondered how brief a viewing must be so that it can be termed a mere glance—perhaps a second or less? Whatever period qualifies, just a few seconds after most sightings, I have unconsciously decided whether something is significant enough to hold my gaze.

Usually my eyes move to another side, but on some occasions my attention is instantly and firmly grasped. A few scenes reappear again and again, not just for seconds, but for many months. Such an experience that has stayed with me for years began with a quick leftward glance one frosty November at the Benedictine monastery near Valyermo in the Mojave Desert.

Two months after the death of my wife Alice, I drove one evening to St. Andrew's Abbey for several days of quiet. I went there partly because there were other places where I did not want to be. I was fleeing from human interaction that had already reached a state of overload. Though at a site which had become very restorative for me during the preceding decade, I was held captive that morning within subtle emotional walls. Grief took a mixture of the urgency for pain to pass and a yearning for good memories to remain, and built a false protective armor, lest pain's departure carry away with it some of the remaining preciousness of a loved one.

Early in the morning after my arrival I walked to a small garden of trees and dried remnants of flowers which lay beyond the guest quarters. On previous visits I had often experienced uplifts of mood while standing or sitting in the quiet garden. On this occasion the numbness seemed impenetrable, and I stayed in motion. Suddenly my attention was seized in the quick glance. A startling brilliance flashed on the sandy ridge rising steeply from the pathway where I hesitated. A large juniper bush seemed afire at the top of the ridge. The shrub shimmered with an intense whiteness, yet was not blinding, and I was able to look directly at it. I stopped, moved backward a step or two, and became absorbed in the scene as my body responded to keep the display in view. There I stood, slowly shifting my posture, first a bow and then a crouch which deepened until finally I knelt with one knee touching the earth. My movement arose not from reverence, but from a desire to maintain the sun, the bush, and my eyes in an alignment that kept the sun out of direct view, yet backlighted the bush.

The juniper bush was not really aflame, I might have confided to a scientific investigator, but such disclosure would have intruded into something more important than rational explanation. I could have mused about a low, just-rising sun, a very gentle breeze stirring ice–covered juniper needles, and the perfect and fortuitous alignment of my eyes with the bush and the sun. By simple reasoning, I could have put aside this chance occurrence and freed myself from the mild discomfort of being unable to explain a simple something about nature. That way I could have also maintained my grief uninterrupted. But a surge of excitement born of the splendor broke through the numbness and pried loose some of my clinging to unhappiness.

Several time in life, I have sensed a perverse momentary comfort in feeling abandoned after the loss of someone or something dear—*if others just knew the depths of my feelings!* But this day the bush kindled a spark which brightly illumined my inner self as well as the spreading plant, and I was lifted out of misery. I forgot to analyze at the moment, and simply let the sight remain glorious.

My journal later reminded me that this was the second time in several weeks when I had literally stopped in my tracks to behold something special in the desert. Two months before, I had paused during another lonely walk to observe and admire a lone, chirping quail, serving dutifully as a sentinel while its fellows fed from the desert floor. I had drawn comfort from that encounter in the simple, but well-received reminder that I was not being abandoned, no more than were the foraging birds. One bird was caring for the other birds the best way I could imagine! If I had dealt fancifully with that event (and mixed several metaphors) I might have considered that the bird was acting quite like the biblical example of a good shepherd—and thereby embellished the encounter with some 'religious' or 'spiritual' significance, whatever that might have added.

On that morning, below the brilliant juniper bush I quickly recollected one of the better-known incidents in the religious tradition that has nurtured my spirit. Burning bush? Why, of course! I recalled how the lawgiver Moses had encountered his God in the radiance of a bush on Mount Horeb. That recollection from my religious heritage gave my awakened imagination a sanction which the birds had not elicited. On his mountain, Moses heard words about holiness: *...put off your shoes from your feet, for the place on which you are standing is holy ground.*

I have asked myself several times why the encounter with a bush touched me more deeply than the quails had done. Had the birds prepared me for a deeper validation to occur below the bush? Did I feel flattered at sunrise because what was presented to me was reminiscent of what had been offered to the mighty Moses? It could have been that the second incident reminded me so much of the scriptural account that my morning experience presumed a validation from scripture: 'When something like this happens it is a real spiritual experience!' Whatever explanations I might have offered, my recollection of the words about holy ground initiated an important deep reflection. Most importantly, I felt included in the promise that the God of Being who cared for Moses, also cared for and would not abandon me.

Today, more than a dozen years since that November morning, I continue to challenge my inclination to accept one thing as holy while considering something else otherwise—at times somehow *less* than holy. Can a place be holy, I inquire, only if earlier authority has pronounced it thus? Is there a further requisite that the place, or object, or person, or encounter must be also *accepted* by a number of human beings who confront that person or place or object? But what are the qualifications of those who pronounce anything to be holy? Does holiness, as beauty has been described, repose in the eye or the mind of the beholder?

My early sentiment after viewing the bright bush was that the place was holy for me, not because it was located on monastery grounds, nor because I had genuflected in a movement which had brought my knee to the earth, but because I was enabled deeply to appropriate a natural splendor. My thinking self yielded to my deep feelings, and I suddenly felt strong and held up by a power which I could not see but knew certainly was present.

9
at home
with holiness

The Abbey reposes in a spaciousness lacking in my home setting. Mountains and sky rising from the desert floor are more than I can embrace in a single visit. I feel docile in this awareness, and must choose between a quick scan of the panorama and a lingering gaze toward the mountains, or along the valley or upward to the clear sky. On this occasion I elect the panorama. My wandering reverie shifts to a settled reverence. I feel attuned to the One who has created the immensity of all that stretches countless light–years in every direction from where I stand. Then a long word pops into my mind as I resume my walk: *transcendence*, naming an attribute of God which goes beyond ordinary experience and even human comprehension.

I realize that I am away from my home. In contrast to this expansive desert place, the small canyon where I live bespeaks an intimacy and coziness. With memory of home lingering, the word *immanence* emerges to suggest the nature of God in a different way. Immanence: the indwelling of God in the world, ever–present divinity.

The words transcendence and immanence rarely arise in general conversation, let alone in combination. I recall their entering my vocabulary during a particular term of theological studies. For a month or more, we classmates unsheathed the weapons of words in friendly duels, presumably to settle the issue of whether God can better be described by transcendent or immanent qualities. I can now admit to having been diffident towards, if not downright impatient with the discussion, though a teaching assistant pointedly suggested that I really should be interested and involved in the debate.

Today I tell myself smugly that my reluctance resided in a desire to know God rather than to know about God. Thus it was surprising that the same words resurfaced as I hiked one morning on the Abbey grounds two decades later. Both words remain in awareness, though they seldom enter my conversation. I am more inclined to know about God than to know or be known by God, for that way I imagine I can maintain control.

But back to school days. Much earlier than the time of our seminary discussions, theologian Rudolph Otto had written *The Idea of the Holy*. His work proved to be a wake-up call for a new day of thought about holiness, though it was sometimes adopted summarily as *the* view to be honored. Otto characterized the religious person's experience of God as encountering a majesty that evokes awesome hesitancy and yet attracts. In school we repeated words such as *mysterium tremendum et fascinans*—describing an experience beyond conception, yet uniquely attractive, so that a person would overall have a strong positive experience. The prophet Isaiah's "Woe is me...my eyes have seen the Lord of hosts!" exemplifies the sudden twofold feeling. So, in a different way, did the high priest Aaron's tedious distinctions between holy and common articles of everyday life in the days of Moses.

In retrospect, I recognize two parts of my internal struggle during these seminary discussions. On the one hand I was warmed by the prospect of friendship with a nearby Jesus, and much preferred that possibility over a remote awesomeness which I could not visualize. But at the same time I hesitated to trust my own simple experiential views alongside what I perceived to be near certainty in a body of academic thought being so animatedly discussed. Mainly I hoped that God would not become so remote as to be absent, yet not so close as to overwhelm me!

Deeper reflection reminds me that for much of my life I have questioned pronouncements that certain places and things and people are holy. Hearing such claims, I could too easily conclude that other places and things and people were not holy. Undervaluing both my own experience and the commonplace, I expected that holy places would lie beyond home. Home remained primarily a place to reside while the parish church and retreat centers provided essential nurture for my spiritual hunger. Still other places would exceed either kind of familiar setting in some imagined spiritual way I could not perceive.

This deeply entrenched supposition lifted gently when my wife Norvene idly wondered whether the oak grove surrounding our house might have been a holy place for Native Americans many years ago. Sharing her wonderment while looking anew at the giant trees bore wonderful fruit! The possibility she suggested warmed my fancy. If I were living tribally a century and a half ago, I should have rejoiced in just such a majestic setting. But would I have lived on soil so acknowledged, or held it in reserve as a place to go for special occasions, as I have tended to do for years?

The valley and the mountains at the Abbey continue to remind me of the incomprehensible greatness of God, and our snug home setting echoes that God is also so near that I can never leave the divine presence. In the desert setting I am reminded of the infinite nature of God, in whose image I am created. The desert's expansiveness becomes a metaphor for an infinitude which I have to claim for myself.

Likewise, I am moved to consider my smallness and vulnerability when I pore over the tiny details of nature on a sandy slope between the mountains, or in my home garden. Quiet meditation lifts up countless thoughts and feelings which keep these discoveries alive in me. I can rejoice when my greatness unites with that of the panoramic scene from the Abbey, or when my smallness and vulnerability find comfort within the embrace of God at home. Most importantly, I find that I truly appropriate these convictions when I am aware of them at the moment of experiencing, and express my perception in some offering of gratefulness.

Nature provides reminders of holiness as truly as those offered by churches, holy wells of Britain, or pilgrimage sites in the Holy Land. Martin Buber has written that holiness penetrates nature without violating it. My comfort in walking and in simply being present to nature, leads me to approach certain sights at random, and I become more and more able to treat reverently what is before me. Whenever I can illuminate from within what I encounter beyond myself, this holiness is made real to me.

I feel warmly about the comment of Oliver Wendell Holmes that all is holy where devotion kneels, in part because I once experienced myself kneeling below a brilliant juniper bush. In a similar epiphany Moses was informed that he was standing on holy ground—clearly and decisively informed, I judge by the conversation which followed. That patriarch was asked to remove his sandals, as I shall be well advised to step out of the views and preconceptions upon which I usually stand.

Now I know that I can put aside long words which both help and hinder when contemplating my relationship with the divine. The God I imagine cannot be adequately described as transcendent or immanent. Nor will a shift from *or* to *and* suffice. But I am playing with words about the imponderable, caught in a mental maze of my own devising!

A morning's south wind swept away my impulse to explain God, as I walked along the highway bordering the north edge of the Abbey land. I was enjoying. Period. No single object accounted for the sense of joy, though earlier that same morning I had hoped to be present to distant things: the full sweep of the small valley, the low crests of two layers of foothills, and the mountains to the south.

It was about nine o'clock in the morning, the sun was well up, and a slight breeze was moving. In an upward glance to admire the light blueness of the sky, I was surprised to behold a bunch of balloons drifting towards me, perhaps a couple of hundred yards above the land. I could distinguish at least six or seven colors in a configuration that might have floated above a salesperson ready to pull a restraining string to extract a chosen color at the time of sale.

"An interesting check on the nature of color," I said, recalling college physics: white light is the sum of all colors (a glass prism separates sunlight into a rainbow spectrum), but black paint approximates the presence of all colors. What, then, was I observing? At first I could make out the several colors: red, yellow, green, blue and others. I continued to walk, pausing every twenty seconds or so to have another look. Meanwhile, the balloons halted their northward progress directly overhead, and rose almost vertically. With the passage of several minutes, I could not verify the colors of the individual balloons. After looking periodically for another five or six minutes, I became aware that above me was a single brilliant light, a bit to bright to be gazed at steadily. Somehow the colors had been recombined. The pigment in the latex of the balloons was no longer controlling the outcome; I had seen a change. My wonderment about holiness that had begun before a sunlit juniper bush came into a new acceptance between sunlit balloons.

All is holy where devotion kneels! The kneeler/beholder becomes part of the creation of holiness. The juniper bush still stands at the crest of the ridge, though now somewhat larger and less compact after a dozen years of growth. I had, in fact, visited it at the same hour of morning only five weeks after the first encounter. My intent was simply to stand quietly in the path below: an expression of devotion with no expectation of witnessing a spectacle. Sure enough, there was no glistening brilliance. The sun on the second occasion was clearly visible through the bush, now an ordinary looking juniper among other juniper bushes.

But there was something new and different this time. Twenty or thirty 'angels' hovered over the bush in an animated dance. The dancers were small. From the distance of a hundred and fifty yards, they appeared the size of softballs or soccer balls, including the halos that encircled them. Curious, but stubbornly unawed on this occasion, I hastened puffingly to the top of the slope, there to behold a number of flying insects orbiting the bush as they were warmed by the brightly rising sun. Larger than gnats, but smaller than house flies, the insects scattered the new light into visible auras enlarged a thousandfold when seen from far away.

I never even bothered to look for flying insects over other bushes in the vicinity, but avowed the possibility that if tiny flies can reflect new sunlight mightily, so could my life reflect the glory of God. Mainly I just felt what I later read as the title of an essay: *Wonder is Such a Sudden Gift.*

10
birds
and bees
and flowers

The large trumpet-shaped flowers bordering my retreat room had lost their pristine whiteness and symmetry overnight. Now in late morning of a hot autumn day, yesterday's white jimsonweed blossoms had taken on light pink hues and shrunken shapes. I marveled that any flower could appear after the dry summer, now a month past, let alone blossoms the size of Easter lilies born on low, rambling plants! But the trumpets were a striking exception among other flowers I discovered as I walked: splashes of yellow on the rabbit brush, but little else.

How diverse the floral offerings had been five months earlier, when springtime flowers adorned the otherwise dull tan and green background. Even then, the beauty had been triggered by moderate winter rain. The Abbey site cozies up to the lee side of the nearby mountains, lying within a partial rain shadow that receives somewhat less water than the high places first visited by storm clouds arriving from the north or west. The mountaintops and their southerly coastal foothills are the main beneficiaries of the moist air moving onshore, diverted upward into cooler air where the moisture condenses to form snow and rain. Yet the moisture had been adequate for scatterings of tiny spring flowers.

In contrast to the Abbey's valley setting, some areas farther inland had been watered generously by clouds that had slipped through mountain passes or over the lower mountains. On those selected desert fields native poppies had burst into an orange–golden carpet so thick that it was virtually impossible to walk in the fields without crushing one or more plants at each step. Flowers of quite different sorts abounded in areas about twenty miles apart, recipients of different amounts of the rain falling several weeks earlier.

Perhaps I was conditioned by the shortage of color on this October day, for two wispy spring flowers especially came to my mind. One is typified by tininess and its suggestive shape and color: a pinkish purple, a ground–hugging miniature version of a bouquet a bridesmaid might carry, yet only two inches across an arrangement of a dozen or more flowers. This plant is but one of several kinds which a hiker can easily bypass, flowers so small and low that they have been humorously termed 'belly blossoms.' An observer needs to stoop or lie on the earth to study their details.

"Why are they here?" I wondered silently, "Why only sparsely here on one of the driest patches of earth around?" Then I realized that the site is probably ideal for these plants for the reason that wetter areas can support larger plants which would overshadow the smaller types and prevent their growth at all.

Thus enlightened, I was not surprised to come across a second unusual type of flower, also in a very barren spot. My impression at first sighting was of small balls of lint, very fine fuzzy leaves in clumps much larger than the thickness of a stem, and flowers so small that I was unaware of them at first. Only when I bent close to the ground could I observe that there were flowers among the fuzz, tiny petals, finely marked with dark stripes. Thread–thin pollen–bearing stamens protruded well out from the flowers, a distance greater than the width of each pattern of petals, slenderly proportioned for the lint–like ambience. Only five or six plants of this kind grew nearby, all within a radius of one or two feet from the plant I first spotted. My brand of photography could not have captured the threadlike intricacy of a clump of the fuzz in its wide array. No, only a good sketch could do justice to this unusual plant. I have drawn a sketch in my memory—and a good thing, for I have not encountered its sort in the several years which have since passed.

I become assertive on recalling Thomas Gray's

Full many a flower is born to blush unseen,
    and waste its sweetness on the desert air.

I want to respond, "Not necessarily so!" And cite examples where I appreciate the beauty as breathtaking. There are carpets of poppies, groves of Joshua trees gesticulating to their companions, and 'Candle of the Lord' yuccas rooted equally well on gentle slopes or recently cut inclines where passing highway drivers may admire their beauty.

These displays grasp my attention, but I know that only a tiny fraction of even the most spectacular flowers are ever admired. The fact of being overlooked is almost universally true of the tiny flowers which lie underfoot. They must be searched for and examined up close. Therein lies a metaphor for the desert: it holds fascinating sights which must be sought out. Is that not true, I ask myself, of much that is beautiful? Is that not true in the divine One and in creation, in my fellow human beings and their offerings, in myself and my efforts?

Flower–seeking in October does not prosper from quick glances. "Where might there be fresh, not–yet–pinkish lilies this morning?" The search presumes patience. A wrong assessment for this particular morning, the journey turned out to be no more than two or three hundred yards. I paused to admire the floral details of the first large rambling jimsonweed plant displaying a dozen or more fresh blossoms. Several bees were active at the scene, and I stood close by for several minutes watching the busy workers. Mainly they were treading the lower inside surface of each trumpet shape, now and again crawling over the dusty stamens extending outward for much of the petal length. I wondered whether the bees were intentionally shaking something from the stamens, to collect it moments later from the which petal surfaces. My question was never resolved, for I could not get close or shift my eyes fast enough to follow their darting flight about and within the ground–hugging plants.

A few paces down the path stood the most colorful (and only other) floral display I could see this day: bushes measuring roughly four feet in each dimension, and well covered with small tufts of yellow florets, somewhat coarser, but gathered in heads resembling dandelions. About forty honeybees were exploring a bush nearby, much more intensely than I had just witnessed on the lilies. No sweetness wasted on this bit of desert air! The bees typically remained upon each carpeted surface for an extended time, foraging over each tuft and periodically pausing to perform some unusual movement which I could not interpret. Then I became aware of bulbous yellow shapes around the second segment of their rear legs, calling to mind the adornment sometimes seen as anklets in Native American ceremonial dances. Each bee bore burdens of the same size and near–spherical shape on its hind legs, some barely visible knobs and others more than an eighth–inch diameter. Apparently balance in flight was not only valued, but attained by the hasty but careful gathering and storing I was beholding. Soon after my arrival, a well-laden bee departed the scene, and then others. But an equal number of replacements arrived. I concluded that the newcomers had delivered their loads of pollen and were now returning to the workplace.

Fascinated to watch such interesting work, and growing in confidence that I could figure out what the bees were doing—and putting aside Winnie the Pooh's caveat that 'you can never tell about bees'—I walked back to the ground–

hugging jimsonweeds. The bees there had not put on their anklets, nor could I explain their busyness. (Pooh was right!) I have since read that bees sip up nectar from deep within some flowers, and that they even gather sticky resin from some trees, but I was not enlightened further by watching particular bees that merely seemed to be walking around on petals and flying from flower to flower.

Five or six hours later, in the heat of the day, I returned to the two plants. As in the morning, there was much activity on the yellow blossoms of the rabbit brush, but none among the now wilted and mostly closed jimsonweed flowers. Several tightly wrapped new bundles would reveal large flowers within the next day or so, but at that time I would be at home miles away.

As if sensing my disappointment, two ravens soared close overhead, claiming my attention as they flew straight for aerial recreation along a well–heated ridge. The day was a fine time to play follow–the–leader, featuring simple dives which the two followed with enthusiasm. Their antics looked quite easy—from my safe observation point on the ground! The ravens drew wings close to their bodies, plunged about ten feet, and flapped just enough to be lifted again by the effort into the uplift of warm rising air, and repeated the procedure time after time along an undulating flight path.

A lone redtail hawk took but one pass along the ridge, and with a wild fluttering of wings came to rest atop a juniper tree. When I turned toward my room, the hawk was still sitting there, perhaps wondering about the earthbound creature who alternately crouched over plants and stood to rub his chin. The ravens had apparently sought fun elsewhere. I was left with several unanswered questions about facts, but with renewed respect for nature's busy creatures—and a sense that they are aware of me.

11
skeletons
abandoned
at a dump

Oh, to be acknowledged as a discoverer! The word evokes images of island landfalls thrusting upward from the sea after a long, despairing voyage, or of a hidden valley below what seemed after days of trailblazing to be just another wooded ridge. Those images from my fanciful side! More realistically, the exciting discoveries in my life rarely come in new, unexplored places off well–trodden ways. Rather, the memorable experiences more often emerge from the familiar. How heartwarming it is to glimpse new expressions on the faces of our children, or the progression of seasonal colors on a favorite tree beyond the kitchen window! So too it is exhilarating to encounter what earlier passings have not revealed in familiar natural settings.

On the spacious monastery grounds I often visit, one pathway around the monks' quarters bypasses the few buildings grouped about the junction of four well–worn asphalt roadways. Like most shortcuts, this back way is simply the sum of several courses favored by drivers of trucks and tractors over an expanse of well–packed sand, now almost devoid of vegetation. The passage of vehicles over the course of years has shaped the way for the future, as diagonal footpaths on school campuses express rejection of more formal square–cornered walkways.

My stroll beyond the buildings began one morning along this back course, though other routes would have provided quicker contacts with 'nature.' I was not three hundred yards from my starting point when I spotted an interesting something just off the compacted bypass. I imagined the skeleton of a miniature cow, and moved towards whatever it was. Only later did I recollect that a cow's skull near a saguaro cactus is a common logo for desert. Involuntarily, I had yielded to the picture of these figures rather than imagining the remains of a smaller object. Right there, the gray–white and compact something, among other thin, bleached objects spread on the earth near a large juniper, suggested the rib–cage of a cow's skeleton.

Imagination raced ahead of examination. The object was in fact plural: scattered remnants of a well–aged automobile storage battery whose white plastic casing had broken open to strew six or eight off–white grids of lead on the sand nearby. Surely the battery had not crawled there to die, but had been delivered to the spot alongside the utility road. My presumption was quickly verified as I spotted a variety of other quite ordinary objects within a radius of six feet: a section of creosoted wood, two white plastic bottle caps, fragments of asphalt shingles, pieces of glass and several shards of earthenware flower pots. Overlooking this assortment was a sheet of aluminum foil, evidently carried by the wind to its present entanglement beyond my reach in the juniper bush.

I could only guess how this mixture of materials got there, and concluded that all except the metal foil had been likely deposited by human hands. I also realized that all of the objects could be classed as non–biodegradable, or nearly so. They were on earth to stay! Several of the materials had established a place in world history because of their usefulness and longevity. Fired earthenware vessels from very ancient times now repose in museums alongside clay objects of cultic worship. Glass has taken a myriad of shapes and usages over the centuries. Asphalt similar to the binder for the fibers in the roofing shingles has preserved ancient papyrus manuscripts for perusal millennia later. And on the sand with these representatives of the past were creations of our time, ubiquitous modern plastics that are forecast to outlast our civilization. Some of the earth's more durable substances were visible in one quick scanning, all within a small area of desert soil.

I have since recalled a quite different encounter with durability here and there within the Abbey grounds. While hiking over a nearby ridge, I encountered distinct impressions in the soil made by the tires of a motorcycle. The markings were well off any path, in a level area where winter rains would be slow to erase the scar. But more impressive than the marks was the offhand remark of a monk to whom I conveyed my newfound information. "Oh yes, a guy rode there about twelve years ago."

The precision of twelve years elapsed is less important than the implied message that the desert is slow to recover from what appears to be mere surface damage. Although relatively few low shrubs might be torn from the soil by a tire's passage, their root structure is also removed in the process, and thereby a means of retaining the surface soil on the sandy slopes. In time, some of the invaded areas quickly become eroded, and visible life disappears. Obviously there is an *inter*dependent way of life across the desert floor! Some plants are dependent upon each other for survival, as are other combinations of life among flora and fauna. This encounter with the imbedded tire tracks made clear the necessity for humankind to cooperate too.

I ponder what is really durable and what is not. When I came upon the abandoned fragments, my attention was claimed by objects which humans have classified as durable—curiously named in an age of planned obsolescence!

Perhaps I focused too quickly on manufactured items, such as the plastics. Indeed, I was drawn by an awareness of the negative impact of the objects, not only about their usefulness but also about human casualness in discarding them. What a shame, I scolded silently, that the inanimate can crowd out the living on the earth!

In my judgmental mode, I initially failed to note examples of permanence immediately before me on the ground. Most evident was the sand itself. Hugging the soil was a tracery of low plants so narrow they seemed leafless. I recalled seeing the same plant type many times in dry locations. There was other quite different life too. Crisscrossing the same small area were many ants busily at their work. To be sure, a given plant or ant could be plucked up or trampled, yet by a generative process each can endure over the ages. Ants are said to have inhabited the earth for more than thirty million years!

But I was focusing on the physical again. Reflecting more widely, it seemed trite to remind myself that love lasts forever; so too friendship and beauty. Yet I admitted there is a profound truth about those familiar values. A lovely sunset will pass within the hour, and an oil painting will disintegrate into dust over centuries, yet an appreciation for beauty is nurtured and extended to future generations by my present valuing. So it is in my honoring the delicate balance of countless living things which constitute what I know as nature.

I reaffirmed on the spot that I want to be part of re-creation. My yearning goes beyond maintaining the natural environment to include human qualities that respect God's creation and God's creatures. I murmured St. Paul's words to the Christians in ancient Philippi:

> Whatever is true, whatever is honorable, whatever is just, whatever is pure, whatever is lovely, whatever is gracious, if there is any excellence, if there is anything worthy of praise, think about these things. *(RSV)*

12
a place
becomes special

Why, I inquire, does the Abbey repose in a special corner of
my heart? For indeed it does. Searching for an explanation,
I assess its natural beauty, the warmth of its resident monks,
and the calming routine of its prayer offices. All contribute
to the affection. I remember the community's attentiveness
when I sought consolation, and recall simple surprises among
nature's offerings. Gifts from both sources quickened my
healing. Gratitude became a permanent resident among my
feelings, and nostalgia continues to beckon as the years pass.

I wonder if I am simply captive to a habit that has built
during a quarter century of visits. This speculation passes as
I acknowledge a childlike expectancy much stronger than
routine or duty, which precedes my visits. While pondering
the special relationship, I begin to suspect that the Abbey
validates my yearning to have and know a comfortable place
in the universe. I know that I would suffer if forever exiled
from either my geographical or spiritual homeland—or
estranged from myself. Each of these factors contributes to
what I deeply feel. I fancy that I have been inoculated by a
few deeply moving experiences at the Abbey, and that my
regular and playful musings continue to nurture what was
initiated in those earlier encounters.

A simple mode of reflection is central to recognizing the
affection I feel. When recollecting an experience, I seek not
only a physical description of what I witness, but also an
opening of myself to perceive and feel below the surface of

what I see or hear or touch. What often begins as curiosity somehow engages me in what I behold, a means of dipping below information that the senses bring to my mind. The outcome is as if three simple questions are posed: What does the object or incident have to tell about itself? What does it have to say about me? What does it impart about its future or mine? A shift occurs from mulling over information, to being engaged in my ongoing spiritual formation.

Perhaps a spotted caterpillar attracts my attention. At first I admire details of the creature, then realize that it began as a small egg, but now voraciously feeds its wormy being. But I also came from a tiny beginning, and much of my feeding is from leaves—of books! I imagine that the crawling thing will become a lovely flying butterfly, and allow that I continue to unfold at all stages of my life.

Or I could be holding a small pebble worn smooth by years of rubbing against other stones in tumbling water. The stone is well rounded, and shows its several colors more brightly in clear water than when dry in the air. I too have been shaped by countless contacts in the external world: I too have preferred settings for revealing my gifts.

This mode of meditation sounds so informal that I seek to name it. Just a few years ago I favored the term *sacramental awareness*, convinced that it is important to look more deeply than the sensual elements of everyday incidents. Within the heritage of the church, I had a ready–made vocabulary about sacramental matters: outward visible signs of inward spiritual grace, for example. But the adjective sacramental suggests a labelling limited to formal religious practices, whereas I regularly encounter a harmony of experience, reflection, and deepened awareness in a wide variety of informal settings. I conclude that what takes place in my reflection is simply respectful or reverential appreciation, worthy of quiet encounter and later recall.

After many four-sided encounters with nature, a hospitable monastic community, myself, and an evident Presence that is beyond and within, I now almost automatically escort part of my consciousness from objects which attract me to a parallel internal inquiry. Thereby I become more open to insights which enrich my meditation. The prompter is not the object alone, but also the memory that there is truly an inner dimension in whatever I behold reflectively. During my childhood, adults probably considered me to be a hopeless daydreamer. I go beyond that view today, using the adjectives *sacramental* and *reverential* to signify that the material offers a spiritual message to a receptive heart, along with an element of mystery that continues to attract me. If I truly feel the sacredness of creation, I am inclined to inquire how it can inform me about my Creator and myself.

My home and the Abbey are especially important to me in this way of perceiving my environment. Home is the place where my wife and I share our lives, where family and friends visit, and where I find comfort and a secure, familiar setting in a neighborhood I have come to trust. It is my primary place. But home also makes demands on me for its upkeep, shelters the telephone that brings both light and intrusive messages, and is the place from which I journey to burdensome work situations. Thus homecomings evoke mixed feelings. On the one hand, I want to defer evening chores that must be dealt with before I can relax. But these feelings are more than countered by the promise of reunion with a loved one and the prospect of creative work that imparts a sense of vitality and of mattering as a human being. Yet despite its richness, I often take our home for granted!

The Abbey transports me beyond the usual to another setting, and beyond myself—a self I also take for granted in the home place taken for granted. While at the Abbey, I am more likely to tend the deep places within myself. For five years or more, I have pondered why this is so. One reason is that I am cared for as an honored guest. And there are a number of other possible explanations. Mainly, however, I have come to realize that my visits there at least briefly remove me from my tendency to *do*, to be active. I even dare to believe that at the monastery I am brought closer to my being than to my doing, closer to my essence.

I find it virtually impossible to convey to my active friends the feeling of simply being. But they sometimes nod in partial understanding when I assert that I am trying to revert from a human doing to a human being. For my own part, I discover bits of direct evidence of the difference between activity and just being when I reach the Abbey. Early during most visits, I act out a transition by hiking for about an hour soon after arriving. On the following days I do not feel the urge to activity I had brought with me. The doing impulse slowly abates.

My home and the Abbey are clearly special places in my life. I accept this reality more and more as I embrace each in a reflective way, revisiting them internally in imagination, prayerful thanksgiving, journaling, and in sharing their importance in conversation with others. My reflective self ('heart' is another name for that self) processes what I have encountered and how I feel about those encounters. So it turns out that there are three centrally important places in my life: home, Abbey, and my heart. A sense of being embraced by any one of the three helps me to value the other two, for my feelings add a valuing dimension of depth which bonds all together.

At times I think that in knowing each place so well, I have learned to know home and the much–visited Abbey 'by heart.' In both settings, I revel in small changes which I could be aware of only given an intimate knowledge of them. I could not appreciate the first spring violets near my house if I had not earlier found their hiding places among much higher vegetation, or exult in the bluebirds returning to the desert, had I not been aware of their long absence. In the words of Martin Buber, I move from I–It relationships to I–Thou relationships, as I let the two places enter my life and move beyond the senses into the heart.

The dual consciousness of external and internal comes in a formal way as I enter the immensity of fine cathedrals or other spaces long venerated by many people whose traditions I honor. An architect friend told me that he suddenly felt the importance of entryways one day, when he visited a Buddhist monastery. To this day, his designs include beautifully crafted elements which signal to a person that she or he is moving from one space to another and is invited to make the internal shift, whether entering 'the holy place' or re–entering 'the world.'

In a practical way, wire fencing about my vegetable gardens minimizes theft of the fruit by passing raccoons, possums and squirrels (the birds are another matter!). But the necessity for garden gates provides visible reminders at each passage that I am moving from one setting to another. I have mused about what might be identified as visible entryways to home and Abbey. For my home, a small driveway bridge provides an imagined but important line of separation between home and non–home. At the Abbey, my major reminder is the act of driving an hour and a quarter from home. The final touch of *I'm here,* is signaled by a small printed sign, just within the monastery grounds: *No Hunting Except for Peace.* For my heart, the threshold is a pause to reflect on how the day has progressed.

I feel a helpful rhythm among the three significant spaces of home, Abbey, and heart. As I call upon all three, I feel supported in a variety of life experiences, whereas to expect the fullness of life from any single one of the three is unrealistic—indeed sets up a dislike for the one. To expect more from my work than it can provide is unrealistic. To call upon a single human relationship is to risk smothering it. The threeness about places is likewise important. I imagine a three–legged stool or tripod that provides stability even where the terrain is rough.

So a threefold view has been helpful to me in seeking the abundant life. I hear rich wisdom as Jesus repeats the great commandments of his upbringing: to love God, and neighbor as oneself—three directions for the love. I know that there is good counsel in the ancient Greek call to be aware of body, mind, and spirit—again a wholeness for each person. I admit my need to honor the divine Trinity, for each of those Persons has touched my life personally.

13
joshua trees

The Abbey lies below the north, inland side of the San Gabriel mountains in southern California. Our home is on the ocean or south side, part way up the same mountains that frame the Los Angeles Basin. The basin side presents several faces of its air from week to week: sometimes clean and bright, at other times smudged by smog. On very clear days I can stand at a street intersection near our house and see the sparkling water of the Pacific Ocean more than thirty miles away, beyond the roofs of the Los Angeles skyline. When skeptical visitors question this claim, I simply point to the name of the street next above our driveway entrance: Poppyfields Street. Oldtime sailors, I am informed, could verify their bearings in springtime by locating the vividly colored fields of native poppies growing in Altadena. My more romantic audiences allow this possibility.

Trips to the Abbey usually follow a curving highway across the mountains, rather than freeways wending their course among the high spots. Poppies are rare along the upper route, but I am rewarded by desert–mountain vegetation that changes with the seasons so faithfully that I can anticipate slight nuances as well as dramatic changes. In springtime, the large blossoms of yuccas are most striking. Since they appear both near the city and in the high desert, I reckon that my homesite would be also desert were it not for water imported for hundreds of miles from the east and north.

The flowering yuccas which first greet me are striking beauties, affectionately, *Candelabas de Dios,* Candles of God, adorning the hillsides. Highly visible in silhouette atop a ridge, they resemble large torches held overhead. Their cream coloring contrasts harmoniously with the tans of the earth and the light greens of lower vegetation. Each plume consists of several hundreds of blossoms gathered in an array about three feet high and half that in diameter, borne upward ten feet or more on stalks issuing from symmetrical half spheres of spiny leaves near the earth's surface.

Proceeding outbound and especially upbound from the coastal basin, another member of the yucca family appears along the highways. This variety, known popularly as the Joshua tree is noteworthy in lacking the symmetry typical of its plumed relative. Indeed, it seems misshapen or ill-planned, for the Joshua points in many directions at once, upward, downward, as well as outward! Poorly planned or not, it is selective about location, thriving above the coastal basin in open woodlands above 2500 feet and higher to about 5000 feet.

The tree's name is credited to Mormons migrating last century from central and eastern states to Utah. Some groups journeyed first in ships, sailing around Cape Horn to California, then moving on foot to the town of San Bernardino and through the Cajon Pass to the high desert. The travelers probably encountered the strange looking trees before reaching the 3100-foot cutoff around the Pass. To a group glad to be ashore after their long voyage, the trees might appear to point toward their promised land. And since the biblical Joshua led another band into a promised land, Joshua trees they came to be named—so goes the legend. Today I relate the shagginess of the trees to my imaginary picture of an ancient biblical prophet, and endorse their name!

Joshua trees are selective about where they will grow, and they did in fact lie in the direction of the travelers' journey last century. The homebound saints might have become discouraged at times, then yet another grove of the pointing trees would appear, and confidence would be restored—so I fancy. Understandably:

> There are some who love it from the moment they first behold it, silhouetted, perhaps, against some desert sunset sky, with the snows of far–off peaks still flashing their signals , and the twilight filled with the last cry of the day birds—the ash–throated flycatchers and plaintive Say phoebes—while nighthawks sweep the skies with pointed wings and the burrowing owls begin to pipe from their holes in the sand. At such a moment the Joshuas lose their gauntness and take on a spiritual quality. With every day that you stay among them they come to seem friendlier and the one right tree in their place. When you have set off again across the treeless spaces of the great Mohave, you greet each rare recurrence of these great Yuccas as a Bedouin greets a palm grove.
> *Donald C. Peattie, A Natural History of Western Trees.*

Close up in daylight, what appeared as fuzziness from a distance is seen to be a thatched covering of rapier–like leaves, one foot or more in length, and needle–sharp. Often several youngsters are found beneath the gesticulating arms of a large tree. The smallest are simple ground–hugging rosettes of sharp spines, while 'adolescents' stand with good posture, like thatched posts. A Joshua tree grows slowly and is a late bloomer. Its first blossom appears at the tip of the straight, upright form, and when this terminal bud dies the initial branch forms sideways, perhaps a foot below the top. Over the years, this manner of forking will continue the asymmetrical shaping that is further complicated as branches break off under their own weight.

The pith within a fallen limb of a Joshua soon weathers away, revealing a tangle of coarse fibers in a hollow structure reminiscent of bamboo stalks. Sometimes a fallen tree displays its full outline, now defined in light–colored fluffy gray dust which remains as a cover while the tree slowly decomposes. I note the absence of annual rings evident in cross-sections of more familiar woody trees. How might I estimate the age of a fallen tree? Only indirectly and approximately, perhaps by the extent of its branching. Claims are made that some specimens live for two or three hundred years.

The blooming and branching are among the less spectacular stages in the life of a Joshua tree. More dramatic events in the tree's life take place on a much smaller scale, notably in how it is pollinated. A tiny moth enters the scene: the yucca moth, technically *Pronuba yuccasella*. This small creature works at night, laying her eggs in the ovary of a flower, where they will soon hatch. This is not an act of casting eggs about indiscriminately. The moth seems quite aware that the larvae will need food as they mature, so she deposits the eggs in the flowers where seeds will form, and upon which the offspring will subsequently feed. Then in a remarkably intentional act by a simple creature, the female proceeds to stuff pollen into the female receptive tube (stigma) of the flower. The larvae will live within the seed pod, consuming a portion of the immature seeds before emerging to fly away as the next generation of moths.

Fruit of the Joshua tree resembles a short lemon cucumber in color and shape, three or four inches in length and about two in diameter. It is internally segmented like an orange, but without a liquid filling. As the cottonwood trees, Joshuas produce a great many seeds, though they are much larger than the cottony lint of their stocky neighbors. In time these fruit pods will dry and separate from the tree, distributing their seeds at random as the pods break open when blown and tumbled by the wind across the desert floor.

Every time I have searched for a perfect seed pod specimen, I have had to admit failure, for each is 'marred' by the action of the small moth. However, this defacing comes with a great gain of a generous number of seeds being fully formed. Indeed, there would be no pollination except by the action of the busy moth. Restated, the Joshua tree forest is dependent upon the moth for its ongoing propagation—and likewise the moth must have the blossoms of the tree to nurture its progeny .

Two quite different forms of life are interdependent in this quiet desert drama. The locale for the ongoing life of each is set by the presence of the other. I begin to seek other similar relationships elsewhere in the world about me, and to value more deeply the nature of true mutuality which pervades all creation

I see my existence as interdependent with others—with people and much more of nature. My uniqueness, which alternates between prideful identity and a basis for humility, comes from beyond myself at birth, and is nurtured or misshapen by the impact of others. I believe that the original person I am (as each other person also is) was known by God before I had the gift of awareness. I yearn to remain in contact with the same God, though the divine ways are often as hidden as the hidden labors of love and creation by a tiny moth in the desert.

14
bright spots
on the rocks

I had walked the same hillside path more than a hundred times
during twenty years of visiting the Abbey. How could I have
failed to see the mosses and lichens growing on rocks not
fifty feet from my well–traveled way? Now back home, I
could think of several possible reasons. Most evident, I used
the path as the quickest route to an uphill objective. Thus
intent upon reaching a goal, I was only generally aware of
details along the way. Then too a panoramic view of the desert
floor lies off to the left of the path beyond a sharp dropoff,
and my eyes drift toward that attraction when not verifying
a safe foothold along the winding path.

But a new factor entered on this day. I was searching for
colors, months after the spring showings, rather than walking
directly to the cemetery overlook. Thus inclined, I wandered
idly into the brush at my right, eyes more alert than usual,
for some mark of color among the neutral earth colors.

The first encouraging signal was a luminous yellow
daubing on a pale gray rock. Moving to the brightness, I
anticipated other markings nearby. Sure enough, small yellow
patches flashed from several directions before I reached the
first bright spot for a close–up look. Small patches of
chartreuse greenish–yellow showed here and there, and more
numerous but less visible mottlings of brown and copper–
red displayed bubbly coatings on rocks of various sizes,
shades, and orientations with the sun. Elsewhere patches of
black appeared smooth as paint, though my fingertips

confirmed a fuzzy texture like bubbly velvet cloth on substantial surfaces of the granite. The most prevalent crusts were off–white, so flaky that they might be easily removed from their anchorage. Not so; they felt hard and well bonded to the rocks! These were the last I noticed: less visible against a background of like–colored rocks, no garish advertising in the subdued color.

These discoveries occurred within a few minutes—after twenty years of my walking past them on a nearby path! Unlike my usual response of jotting a brief note, or counting and measuring at the site of something new, I prowled slowly about the slope among large juniper shrubs and boulders, stepping around low plants now devoid of their summer blossoms, browsing. Truth to tell, I would have needed a strong magnifying glass to examine the rock–hugging growth, and help from the recorded knowledge of others.

I now realize that I had long assumed the natural habitats for lichens and mosses to be damp forest and meadows, not dry deserts. Here before me was evidence to the contrary. Surprises continued to emerge as I moved from my own probing to written sources. These simple forms of life can survive year–round arctic conditions, or on windswept alpine crags, or on slopes newly devastated by volcanic eruptions. Even Main Street USA displays patches of lichens and a variety of related mosses.

In the subsequent two or three weeks, several excursions through the nearby public library confirmed my suspicion that lichens constitute a very basic step in the evolutionary process of plant development and indeed of soil formation:

> …the smallest crustaceous lichens begin to cover these arid rocks, and are sustained by minute quantities of soil, and imperceptible particles brought to them by rain and by the atmosphere. These lichens in time become converted by decay into a thin layer of humus…
>
> *John H. Bland, Forests of Lilliput*

The naturalist Carolus Linnaeus also made this observation more than two hundred years ago. That is approximately half the length of time required for the formation of one inch of humus under conditions where much more organic material is available than in the desert setting.

One of the most startling facts about lichens is that their structure consists of two very simple forms of plant life: algae and fungi bound together in a very loose structure. The fungal framework of the composite resembles a tiny version of filaments that form plastic kitchen scouring pads.. Algae dwell within this loose tangle. They are very simple plants of a quite different sort. The algae contain chlorophyll, and in the presence of sunlight can produce needed nutrients. In contrast, the filamentary fungi are unable to manufacture food, but must depend upon the products of organic decay absorbed from the immediate surroundings, or parasitically, if bonded to a living host.

Both of these life forms abound in nature: algae exemplified by pond scum or ocean seaweeds, and fungi by molds and mushrooms. My familiarity with each recalled only damp places, yet on a morning hike I encountered them in the dry desert, bound together in an intimate relationship of survival.

I imagine that the porous network of lichen, no thicker than a common coin, captures tiny bits of pollen or animal matter transported by air currents. Though the roughly spherical algae accept the hospitality of the supporting structure, they are the hosts in providing nourishment. Seemingly imprisoned by the threadlike fungi, the algae in fact find safe anchorage in the fibers, protected from injury and shaded from excessive sunlight. The tough mat of fungal material provides a bonus for the algae. Being gelatinous, the filaments can retain water in times of drought, and this water is essential for food production.

Some scientists argue that the fungal component in fact lives as a parasite upon the fragile algae, noting that tiny feeding tubes extend from the fungi into the algae—perhaps signifying that the latter is higher in the chain of life. Others argue for symbiosis or shared living. Such wondering notwithstanding, there seems little 'objection' from either living resident, for some colonies of lichens are believed to have lived in such interdependency for 2000 years!

Musing about the simple lichens, I recognize many other examples of mutualism in the life–cycle of plants and animals. Broccoli leaves in my garden are common pastures to which ants carry aphids that then produce a milk–like food for the ant colony many yards distant. In flower beds and on fruit trees, I observe honeybees gathering pollen, all the while pollinating blossoms in their unintentional brushing movements. In the Caribbean Sea, I have been fascinated by the tiny goby fish keeping station in specific locations to which much larger fish come and submit themselves to parasites being cleaned from their gills.

True mutuality improves the quality of life. With the lichens, interdependency is clearly necessary for survival. I acknowledge the essential relationship between humans and the many elements of nature, reminding myself that I am utterly dependent upon air and water and foodstuffs, and much more. Clean air might not be a directly perceived necessity at my home, except when the smog becomes intense; but its clarity increases the enjoyment of what I can see at very great distances in the desert. I appreciate water as a spectacle when its movement reflects the sunlight or throws up wild foam, and only after the playfulness thirst reminds me to see it as necessary for my survival.

I delight in nature especially where it is least disturbed by human intrusion, hence my affection for the desert grows as city life becomes more congested and contrived. My ongoing response is to seek more and more how I can shape not only the possibility of survival of nature but also the quality of existence. I continue to be shaped by valuing a twofold way of seeing the Earth: childlike in exploration and wonder, yet honest and decisive in facing the hard facts of living both on and from the Earth. What I come to hold in reverence

> depends on the grandeur of the earth. The mystery of things impinges upon us because we have such a gorgeous planet. If we lived on the moon, our sense of the divine would reflect the lunar landscape. Our imagination would be empty, our emotions would be dull, our intelligence wouldn't be anything to name— or very little—and because we wouldn't have an outer life we wouldn't have an inner life.
> *Thomas Berry, 'Saving the Earth'/Fellowship in Prayer.*

Out of the mildly embarrassing experience of discovering the lichens only after years of passing them by, I wonder whether I am missing foundational elements in the way I go about appreciating my life. One temptation for an achievement- oriented person is to set a goal and reach it. Now I find it possible also to enjoy the journey. Brother Lawrence counseled this long ago in *The Practice of the Presence of God,* but I forgot! As I readjust my pace, I look for what else I am missing from the treasury of living in harmony with my surroundings.

How fundamental to the soil of the Earth are the simple creatures which slowly replace what is harshly removed! Time and persistence are their nature; I need intentional control of my many impulses. As lichens are building blocks for the Earth's crust, attentiveness can be a sound basis for my continuing spiritual growth. That will involve all of me more and more as I realize over and over that I cannot separate my body or mind from the rest of me. But I am slow to become aware!

15
daily prayers
in the desert

Through the mysterious channel of memory, I crisscross the seven hundred acres of St. Andrew's Abbey while sitting at home. I realize that nature has been both my teacher and a mirror reflecting personalized offering: small rock–hugging patches of lichens seen in bright daylight, Joshua trees eerily backlighted by a half–moon, a creek that bubbles noisily for some distance and then disappears, and bright stars alongside the wide, white band of the Milky Way. Scampering quails have comforted me and my imagination has soared with high–flying hawks. While exploring the creek's valley and the low hills, my vision rhythmically moves in three directions: upward toward the nearby mountains, downward to small objects underfoot, and inward to my own musing. This threefold rhythm during the hikes about the Abbey grounds has enriched my life.

But credit for periodic restoration cannot be given only to the natural setting. Quite as helpful are the twenty monks and lay associates who reside at the Abbey. The monks live in a particular way under the Rule of St. Benedict. As their gift to others, they have chosen to maintain a setting where people can come for refreshment. Their fifth century founder required his community to greet a guest as they would welcome Christ. I am one of the many latter day beneficiaries of his warm counsel.

The story of this monastic community began in Belgium, from where a group when as missionaries to the Szechwan province of China. After a few years there, a harsh blow came in the mid–1950s when the communist forces evicted them. Through one of their number studying in America, they found Hidden Springs Ranch near Valyermo in the Mojave Desert and purchased it as their home. The ranch became St. Andrew's Abbey.

Since moving to California, the monks have increased in number, and the grounds and structures have also changed. Buildings now fit sensitively into the natural setting as the monks' presence has quietly joined the larger community of the Antelope Valley. Some existing ranch buildings were adapted to new uses, and others were added. The chapel was formerly the ranch stable, and the gift shop and bookstore was a two–car garage. Two long guest houses were constructed apart from a new monastic enclosure. An acre of dry land became a bright green meditation garden of trees, flowers and lawn. Spacious ranch sheds were transformed into dormitories of a youth center, and a scout camp without building was laid out farther up the road. The entire land is designated a bird sanctuary, though spent shotgun shells at the far end of the property reveal that trespassers have violated this intention.

In reading historical accounts about monastic communities that have existed over the centuries, I am especially struck by their health–giving influence on society during what is commonly called the Dark Ages, say the fifth through the eleventh centuries. I believe it is a fair appraisal that western civilization was preserved, likely also greatly advanced, during that period by schools, shops, libraries, hospitals, orphanages and hostels. Most were created and maintained by men and women committed to a monastic life expressed in community rather than the solitary hermit's mode. I ponder what the Abbey in the Mojave Desert consistently preserves in modern society, and tally mainly a quiet setting away from urban busyness, persons offering counsel for those whose lives are difficult, and overall the model of a life style contrasting with how most people exist today.

The principal work of the community is prayer, which both eases and intervenes in the work of hands and minds when the chapel bell *Raphael* summons the community on four of the five daily occasions for prayer. It has been well said that the monks in earlier centuries kept the lamp of charity burning for society in their singing of praises and prayers, and so it seems today at the Abbey.

Benedictines live in community, shaping a spirituality of human life in harmony with nature, not shunning abundance but enjoying a middle way between denial and waste, between hoarding and rejecting material blessings of the earth. Benedict encouraged balance in life, so that body, mind and spirit are all nurtured and expressed. I feel most in harmony with myself and others when living within limits I have willingly accepted. Those chosen boundaries are most helpful when they are firm but not rigid, and have been tested by many people over the centuries.

The distillation of Benedictine life is summarized in the *Rule of St. Benedict;* perhaps more finely so in the three vows of stability, obedience, and conversion of life. The vow of stability, in contrast with mobility, is to remain in the same place and membership until and unless a group is delegated to move elsewhere for new work. Someone outside the community hearing this for the first time might exclaim to a monk: "Do I hear you saying that you have promised to remain with the same group of men on those seven hundred acres for the rest of your life? Have you really thought through your decision?" A quick response might be, "Well, I figure that if I can't encounter God here, what's to say that I can do so anywhere?"

My personal response to the concept of stability is to maintain an ongoing contact with a single place which counters the busy area in which I live. I do not need to figure out the details and the ground rules for a succession of places where I might seek quiet. Consequently, I can shift almost immediately into the relaxation which I seek, in a setting I have come to know intimately. I wonder if this is true because I leave a part of myself at the Abbey at the end of each visit, so that each return is not only a reunion with the place and its residents, but also with that part of myself which I left there in trust. In any case, I can be present to what is familiar but ever changing, and appropriate many facets of what is before me. This is a form of stability which I can practice, though I am not a permanent resident of the community. The unexpected reward is that more and more I discover that God is there and here, at the Abbey and in my home.

The vow of obedience seems at first hearing to be old-fashioned, for a common modern goal is individualism or assertiveness above all else! But there are two primary meanings of the word 'obedience' in the monastic sense, neither of them meaning blind compliance. The first is to obey elected authority of the community, whose leaders are guided by the Rule to be sensitive and just. In part, this means accepting some details that might be individually uncontrollable. (Now and again I remind myself that I cannot single-handedly bear total responsibility for everything around me anyhow!) A second meaning of obedience is deep listening, a prerequisite to knowing either myself or the world in which I live. My best practice is to discover that gentle treatment of both subject (myself) and object (what I am beholding or hearing) adds a spiritual dimension to creation as I encounter it.

Obviously, stability and obedience are not easily separable. I cannot be obedient to my quiet self if I am constantly in motion, physically or otherwise. So too is a third vow closely connected to the other two: the vow to accept ongoing conversion of life in the monastic setting.

This vow summarizes the practical test of community: letting my life be changed, guided by a vow of openness which entails the risk of being transformed while living in community, guided by the Rule and tested daily by the give and take of being with others.

I believe that a monastic family would be a good laboratory for researching what constitutes authentic human community. Though the subject is beyond my competence, several issues are evident. Fundamental is the need for support which allows life together in a way that maintains solidarity of the group without submerging the significance of each individual. For this there need to be guidelines to which all members of the community subscribe, and some formal organization having an intentional elasticity. The guiding document for the community is the sixth-century Rule, necessarily under constant review, and being adapted to contemporary circumstances.

Several insights from the Rule are pertinent to life today. The salutary influence of balance or measure in life is emphasized: activity and reflection; solitude and relationship with others; work, study and prayer—in short, concern for the whole person, body, mind and spirit. A second lesson for me is that I live most fully when my choices are conscious and sustained. In the community, vows are not expected or received until an aspirant has had several years to weigh the mixture of commitment and freedom which go hand in hand. A similar deliberation needs to be honored in life lived apart from the Abbey. Finally, the Rule gives a refreshing view of material things: the tools of the gardener are to be considered as sacred as the vessels at the center of the altar. The common things of the storeroom or woodland can be true channels of God's revelation.

St. Benedict called his community 'A school for the Lord's service.' Although not living in the community, I feel that I am the beneficiary of interaction with the people and their tradition, by being cared for, and practicing rhythm in my life. Regular meditation and journaling help me to counter the much louder voices which emerge from living an active life in a busy metropolitan center. Learning in this school lies beyond cognition, for here I can learn by heart—where my heart draws me regularly to be present at a very special oasis.

16
the desert
and my spirit

The desert I have come to know is certainly not static! Land contours are modified from year to year at the urging of wind and water. Plants change in the course of a short season from bright to muted shades, in time blending with the hues of the earth to which their substance also returns. Landscape tinting shifts hourly as the sun traces its path: from grays to light tans, then to browns and purples. With all this change the desert creatures are patient as they await renewal. Seeds lie ungerminated for years, and creek beds remain dry until freshened by water from the heights. So also some animals are dormant for long periods, hibernating in cold winter or estivating during summer's heat. There is no rush to move quickly to the next stage in life.

Human beings have also adapted to desert variations over the ages. In early biblical times, nomadic life was the natural way for Abraham and Sarah, as indeed it remains for the Bedouin people today. I fancy John the Baptist, fifteen hundred years after Abraham, traversing the dry regions and interacting with more settled people near the desert fringes. Jesus retreated to the desert for forty days of solitary assessment after his baptism by John. An Essene monastic community lived near the Dead Sea at about the same time, so we learn from their writings which were remarkably preserved until discovered this century. Just a few centuries after the Essenes, Antony was widely known among many who chose the hermit's way of life. The desert has been surprisingly hospitable to those learning its rhythms and idiosyncrasies.

Several inducements and motives have beckoned the desert fathers and mothers. One incentive was to get away from attractive places that can divert would–be hermits from their primary search for intimate relationship with God. This rejection of attractiveness sounds strange today, but some people then viewed violent society as a virtual shipwreck from which to flee for dear life. Even when active persecution and martyrdom of Christians had largely ceased, the more fervent believers sought austere living as a way at least to approach martyrdom in the name of the Lord. Still other ascetics living far from desert regions refused to be deprived of the experience of being apart, as Irish monks demonstrated by withdrawing to the lonely seas in search of the Isles of the Blessed.

In recent centuries, the term *desert spirituality* has come to signify a particular view and life style. Solitude is one major element, and simplicity of setting is another. Created things and the actions of society are avoided because societal pressures slowly mold one into an inauthentic self and distract from the goal of union with God. One current image of a desert hermit is as a mysterious loner whose unusual life style is incomprehensible to the general populace. But the central distinction for this mode of life is traditionally more a matter of commitment than of anything else, specifically a commitment to shun what attracts the senses, in order to be attentive to inner movements of the spirit.

Desert locations provide physical separation from the lures, and a solitary setting for continuing a patient search for relationship with God. Sometimes the person is transformed by the experience:

> ...solitude molds self righteous people into gentle, caring, forgiving persons who are so deeply convinced

84

of their own great sinfulness and so fully aware of God's even greater mercy that their life itself becomes ministry. In such ministry there is hardly any difference left between doing and being. When we are filled with God's merciful presence, we can do nothing other than minister because our whole being witnesses to the light that has come into the darkness.

Henri Nouwen, The Way of the Heart.

I would not succeed as a hermit! Though appreciating quiet retreats that minimize activities and interactions with others, I would fret if deprived of communication with fellow human beings for months on end. Physical barrenness would be another burden, for I am accustomed to nature's beauty. Nature truly nurtures me, so I immerse myself in it rather than push it aside. In the desert scarcity I must seek the fine details, and can be more attentive than in other settings where my senses almost shut down with the overload. There my senses mediate a richness of creation and initiate a feeling of attunement with my Creator.

Openness to savoring nature, rather than putting it aside as a distraction, has been termed *mountain spirituality.* As the desert is the scene of important biblical events, so are the high places. On Mount Sinai within its awesome smoke, Moses receives stone tablets on which the ten commandments are written. Elijah flees there for safety, and is given a surprising new outlook on life. Jesus finds seclusion for solitary reflection and for teaching his followers in the quiet places. A major mark of these examples of spiritual refreshment is that something is received. Because initially the central dynamic is not commitment, high moments on the mountain occur during relatively short periods within the framework of ongoing life. Worship at the high places in biblical times acted out the belief that something could be received from the liturgies.

I imagine several reasons for the popularity of mountain spirituality. Practically, the rarefied air helps me to slow down physical activity. In a quite different direction, persons in every age have been convinced that a mountain top is closer to 'heaven,' and accordingly selected high places as their altar sites. In biblical times, this inclination might be prompted by volcanic rumblings that suggested the awesomeness of the God associated with the place.

Much less daring, I welcome a hike in the nearby mountains to get myself out of and above the smog, literal and figurative. But I also find that becoming in tune with nature is possible—in a variety of settings—when I am receptive. Wherever I am open and expectant, I receive the gifts of insights breaking into my awareness surprisingly and delightfully as I attend to details of natural creation. In their way of popping into my quiet mood, these gifts of intuition, images, new questions to ponder, and the occasional metaphors, are accompanied by an element of mystery—as if they have been awaiting a moment when I can deal with them respectfully. The central factor is not so much the content of what is suddenly perceived, but that I make myself available to receive newness.

For several centuries what I experience in quiet musing has been termed in the positive way: saying 'Yes' to what the senses bring to awareness. The word *kataphatic* is used to describe this way: being presented to the mind *together with* what is revealed by the senses—insight along with a sighting, for example. A tightly wrapped rosebud leads me to consider that at that moment I am tightly confined within my own concerns, but also that I have the potential to be open to new light.

In contrast to this mode of searching through the matter of creation, desert spirituality is termed the negative way: negating the senses in order to receive from another part of the consciousness. The word *apophatic* describes this approach: far from, or moving beyond objects or human senses. Thus intentional participation in encounters with God is seen as dependent upon negation of self and its efforts to control access to the Divine Being. If the central mark of desert spirituality is commitment, and I consent to be shaped in that way, I might practice a new valuing of ongoing commitment to my marriage, or make room in my other activities to nurture a needy segment of society.

The name for a preferred type of spirituality is not the issue. Both desert and mountain spirituality are terms accepted enough to appear in current writings. One is not better than the other, and I remind myself that the naming is quite arbitrary.

As I ponder how my spiritual hunger might be alleviated, I turn to a metaphor which recalls silver mining in the Mojave Desert. I imagine an underground vein of silver from which a few early miners have already extracted a worthwhile quantity of the metal. Other prospectors converge on the scene to seek their wealth. Some newcomers sink vertical shafts. Others dig horizontally into a hillside. Still others direct powerful jets of water to wash away the soil and expose the metal. All seek the same vein of precious ore, yet their means vary. So it is, I believe, in the various Christian 'spiritualities' which have acquired names over the years. What they have in common is the search for a treasure, and not their methods for reaching it.

In truth, I find that the basic elements which nurture me in a retreat experience cannot be comfortably termed either 'desert' or 'mountain' spirituality. In my trips to the desert site snugly resting against a mountain, I simply try to move beyond activism and settle into a place of quiet within myself. Others have chosen to do this in hermitages, some while on pilgrimages. Much of the time a fact of life is that I cannot withdraw at will from my working environment. Thus constrained at home or wherever else I happen to be, I simply do what nourishes me spiritually as well as physically and mentally: mini–size getting away, as it were. The fundamental place of retreat then, is within my heart. The more I recognize this reality, the more I make room for God's presence, and my awareness that the divine truly enters my life in the everyday.

17
taking time
to ruminate

I dare not state emphatically that I like deserts—period. That assertion would not bear up well under testing. Truth to tell, the desert land I know represents just a fraction of a single nearby desert, itself tiny in contrast with the statistic that one–third of the earth's land is desert!

Nor can I say that I like or choose desert–dry experiences in my life, even though much personal growth has come out of those seemingly barren periods. Helpful or not in the long run, life's deserts are uncomfortable. I neither ask for encores nor claim that they are good things!

On the other hand, repeated visits to a desert place of my own choosing have rewarded me as I have learned things about it and myself before familiarity developed. My continuing desire to frequent the Abbey signals a relationship that has grown beyond mere acquaintance, a shift from impersonal I–It to a personal I–Thou relationship. My regard for self has also prospered. I cannot describe in detail how either shift has occurred, but both involve learning details about a particular oasis rather than holding an unexamined general image of desert. I know also that the process has involved allowing common things to express holiness.

Two elements converge in my perception and valuing of outward and inward encounters at the Abbey. First, the physical setting is a monastery; second, the way life is lived in a monastic community provides a model for my musing about changes within myself. I especially value the three Benedictine vows of stability, obedience, and conversion of life. Pursuing this insight periodically as experiences deepen my appreciation, I recognize that frequent visits to a single place establish a known and secure base from which my personal explorations may proceed with a sense of stability radiating into all of my outlook. A growing two–aspect familiarity with the natural setting and with my own spirit leads me to scrutinize both the place and my outlook: a new and personal view of obedience in the sense of deep listening. From that attitude of presence emerges an expanding openness to incidents and reflection in daily life, complete with the possibility of my being changed: a growing awareness of slow and gentle conversion of life. The spiritual dimensions of my life deepen as I honor simple everyday experiences in times of meditation. From this daily practice, I realize that I have in fact made a commitment to ongoing, lifelong spiritual growth. This is the nature of my spiritual formation: a slow movement in relationship with God, rather than a movement deeper and deeper into my unexamined cravings.

Small details of experiences at the abbey have been very important, though their impact varies when they arrive. Some have proved to be distinct turning points: the quail assuring me that I was not forgotten in my grief, the burning bush opening a perception of holiness as I accepted that possibility increasingly about simple objects of creation. Other less spectacular encounters have resided within me to become enduring insights. The creek which disappears and resurfaces, comes to mind when I am tempted to abandon patient waiting in the face of complex issues. The sparseness of flowers growing widely spread out, counsels me to limit my expenditure of energy—and even of animating creativity— to a level that can be nurtured: a good advisory when I tend to overextend!

I see a direction in the movement of my spiritual quest. In a philosophical mood, I trace four stages of attraction and commitment to a particular monastic oasis. The first echoes Joseph Wood Krutch's comment that long before he ever saw the desert he was aware of the mystical overtones which the observation of nature made audible.

I recall one important pointer to be the timely convergence of an essay about desert spirituality and my search for a deeper knowledge of God. Plain curiosity to know more about God's creation in the ordinary things around me was of much longer standing. It persisted from childhood. Those two elements share credit for the invitation to explore desert of land and desert of self.

The second stage in attraction to the Abbey has been enchantment: being captured by objects of creation which repose in their God–given way in the world about me. After a while I sense excitement upon encountering newness that emerges in what has become familiar. Desert lichens and mosses initiated a firsthand examination, followed by later perusal of what others have recorded about these intriguing restorers of the soil. I have profited by contact with the lichens and the wisdom of others who have studied their simple life.

Within myself, I am equally captivated to learn new things about my longtime marriage partner. As is true for other explorations, that relationship grows by what we experience together and what has been shared by others who have thought deeply about the mystery of marriage. An element of excitement is truly there, not only because each discovery adds information and promise, but also because I realize that both the marriage and I continue to grow spiritually and humanly. The information gained is directly connected with my formation at any age. That perception adds expectancy about a future continuity which extends beyond the present.

I believe that the third step in my desert oasis journey has been a to–the–bones–and–heart acceptance of the sacredness of creation. The focus is almost atomic in the details, and universal in the generalities which can be applied to my life. Quickened in either direction, I feel freed to perceive a dimension deeper than the surface experiences of life. I used to be amused that St. Paul's Letter to the Ephesians lists four dimension instead of the usual three: breadth, length, height and depth! Today I want to claim the sacramental dimension as the fourth, lying beyond the three of geometrical space. That dimension says there's more to it (whatever *it* may be) than can be measured or perceived by senses alone. Instead of struggling to understand by reasoning, I muse about a plant's growth: rooted and reaching downward into the hidden parts of the earth for water and nutrients while at the same time reaching upwards to the sunlight. I recognize a two–directional necessity to reach inward as well as outward in my own life. That reaching may take many forms, some of which bear the commendation of pioneers in the spiritual quest.

A fourth element frequently drawing me back to any place of which I am fond, is the warm mixture of the memories of what I have earlier experienced there, and a yearning to make future journeys to the site. The feeling is like nostalgia and it is quite specific. I can recall the strong urge I felt years ago to revisit my boyhood city in Kentucky. Before leaving home, I shared with friends that I was going for a visit to the city. I now know that I sought not to return to the place in some general sense, but rather to have another look at specifics. In particular there were two schools I had attended, the bank of a creek alongside which my family had lived for several years, a farm where I had worked, and the city's Ohio River waterfront. Because my focus was on specific places in the town, I concluded that important insights and feelings were associated with the details, that certain experiences occurred at and cannot be separated from those places. Places are important at all stages of life, not simply as locations where I exist, but because they become part of me in a mysterious but very real way.

From my collage of journeys and reunions, relaxation and insights, reflections and feelings, the most treasured and surprising realization for me is that I am given a sense of fulfillment about my existence. Life is more whole. What had been missing is provided, even if it seemed trivial at the time, or remained unidentified. I become the point of a convergence of external and internal offerings. I am taught by the blend of an incident and the desire to write about it in my journal or otherwise to search my interior as well as the object or event encountered outwardly. My awareness becomes itself a welcomed oasis.

How does this awareness come about? My immediate response is 'gracefully.' But I also know that I repeatedly invest in a process which begins most easily when I set aside usual activities, for they often both produce and limit. In the combination of commitment and relaxed attitude, I am easily captured by the simple thoughts which come during a walk or while I am sitting quietly. By temperament, I am given to wonder, hence speculation about what I am experiencing may be either playful fancy or serious pondering. I do not hesitate to inquire silently of a busy bee or a flower bud, 'What can you tell me about me?' I find that simple, noncompetitive creatures are very cooperative and informative!

I seldom pause to ask myself how all of this is integrated with my life, for I have become willing to let newness find its place in me, as any new acquaintance may or may not become a friendship. I recall Paul Tournier's counsel, "We remain a stranger to the place we are in, or integrate ourselves into it." He was speaking about physical locations, but I find that the same applies to my own being. If I do not integrate my spirit with my existence, I remain a stranger to my spirit!

Overall. I realize that I am open to the practice of receptivity, and this is analogous to monastic hospitality. I fancy that St. Benedict might have written: "Receive this insight as you would a word from Christ."

18
rainbows and other
heavenly visions

A soaring spectral arch framed the lower end of the valley, resting upon distant ridges of earth to my left and right. Its several colors blended sequentially into each other, red along the outer curve and light purple inside. The bow was almost a half–circle, as natural rainbows are when the sun is near rising or setting. How big was it? Very! How high... how far away... how thick toward the east... how long would it last? I couldn't answer any of those questions.

I did confirm that the sun was bright and well toward its setting. A rain shower that had driven me indoors a half–hour earlier passed and left the air much cooler. As the sun warmed my back and the colors of my imagination, I realized that my role in the drama was to place myself between the two and look away from the sun. And since I was not gazing sunward, what I saw must be reflected sunlight transformed in the east and sent back toward the sun and my eyes in an array of quite different colors.

The curved bands were both bright and fuzzy. The outer band of red gave way to a stripe of orange after first mixing with it, and in turn to yellow, green and blue—though I needed both present and past knowledge to assure myself that seven colors were actually displayed. Boyhood tinkering with the inner workings of radios and their color–coded components advised me that the final shift inward from blue is first to indigo and finally to violet, descriptive words seldom used today. "Remember, boys: Mr. Roy G. Biv: red, orange, yellow, green, blue, indigo and violet..." helped me sort the merged hues. My enjoyment was partially informed by what observers before me had ascertained. These unknown people supplied some of the detail I was aware of while enjoying the rainbow! Even so, I was not sure that the standard seven colors were all there, but the spectacle was enough in itself.

Where was the rainbow? It was out there and yet it did not exist, at least not in the single plane as it appeared. Its colors were emanating from individual drops of rain still falling in the thundershower then moving in a mass well away from where I stood. Individual droplets of water, millions of them, were serving as combined prisms and mirrors. Invisible 'white' light from the sun entering each individual droplet was separated at the interface of air–water into the colors appearing in the bow. But for my eyes to take in the splendor, that color–refracted light had first to reflect from the far inside of the droplets and head back towards where I stood. Not quite directly, however, for the spectrum of light was again divided on exiting the droplet into the less dense air. The sunlight entered each droplet and was reflected from countless water–air inward surfaces to emerge in a band which represented only a few angular degrees that included my line of vision.

And why the bow shape? Why was the color distributed in a wide arc, with none showing in the vast central portion? I judge it so because sunlight entering a droplet straight along a raindrop's radius would simply pass through, or be reflected backwards at an angle that would not include where I stood. I was seeing the refracted light from what had entered droplets near their sides. A tiny part of the sunlight was coming back to be seen in divided colors, yet the overall result was most impressive.

There are so many spectacles in the atmosphere! Most are silent and harmless, and unexpected. The late afternoon rainbow rested patiently on its foothill supports long enough for me to invite others to enjoy the loveliness. In contrast, the sharp rattling of thunder following an unannounced lightning flash had urged me to seek cover a half hour ago. So much of nature's energy being released in a short time, that all people around were aware!

Some of the atmosphere's optical tricks come so quietly that I scarcely divert my gaze toward them. Heat waves above the highway pavement are commonplace in the desert. But now and then their cousin mirages dangle inverted trees and structures suspended in the air, challenging discovery of their source. (I have never met the challenge!)

Some nights I behold a halo or corona framing the moon—atmospheric ice crystals refracting the light, I am told. On occasion I see a reddish color on the inner edge; always, however, I am unwittingly at the vertex of the optical display. I can behold the spectacle only because both what I see and my eyes are properly placed at the moment.

I have been frightened by some aerial displays, and mystified by most. Lightning evokes awe because I know that it comes from electrical discharges more powerful than my mind can comprehend. Those sharp sounds startle me. A less bombastic aurora borealis has seemed eerie to my unaccustomed eyes. Did I actually hear and see it simultaneously from points in Canada and Alaska—but how can one hear light?

Most awesome was a faint blue flame–light which appeared quietly during a very early morning watch aboard a naval ship as I was standing deck duty. Cables along the catwalks, radio antennae, mast and yardarms all emanated an eerie–colored something eight inches or so thick around them. Could this light be seen from a hostile submarine which might surface nearby? That threat seemed unlikely, but so did the experience itself! And I became an instant hero on that occasion, thanks to adventure stories read a decade or more earlier. "It's St. Elmo's Fire—and not in a story book!"

How privileged yet mildly unnerving are these spectral encounters! And how I once felt that I had been accepted into an exclusive group after an ever–so–quick viewing of another sight. At sunset on a day which I have recorded in my journal as surely as I should have done about a hole–in-one at golf, I was gazing idly toward the ocean horizon from a hilltop. Truly as quick as a wink, the just sinking sun showed forth the fabled green flash! I have since heard both explanations and refutations of this phenomenon. When I begin to doubt, I simply check with yet another airline pilot who has likely beheld a similar spectacle. Yes, I saw it! And I no longer feel that I need to defend the experience.

Atmospheric optics, angels, halos: receptivity of the viewer is involved along with whatever else is happening at the time. A former acquaintance purported to have a gift of seeing auras about the heads of other people. "Your aura is reddish this morning. Are you getting enough rest?" This was my introduction to what she saw about me. A few days later it was more comforting: "Your aura is pale blue today— good!"

What am I to make of these experiences? My response will vary from year to year. I am tempted to draw some sort of moral from what I have seen. Better yet, I rejoice in the realization that I have actually moved beyond the enjoyment of nature's spectacles. Sometimes I am quite aware, right then, that I am enjoying. That adds greatly to the pleasure. I learn that I see special gifts when I am most receptive, and that there is a thin line between the scientific and the mystical. The quicker–than–a–second green flash reminds me that I can draw upon the wisdom and experience of others, while holding true to what has been given specially to me.

19
a high
in the high desert

What a wonderful morning, I judged while hiking in crisp autumn air of the high desert. I felt no burden of unfinished chores looming in the background, breakfast had been substantial, my shoes felt comfortable, and a favorite walking stick was in hand. Quick probing of a jacket pocket confirmed the presence of a pen and card, in case I later wished to jot a few notes.

I was, in fact, already in motion when these several confirmations came unpremeditated. My memory was also idly stepping through other settings which I had savored in the past. A long-forgotten building emerged in images from my childhood: The Fun House which several times had challenged and amused me into happy young hysterics. The building's front wall boasted several bright colors, and its doorway broadcast deep, rollicking laughter to prospective visitors. Beyond the ticket counter, an entry bridge lurched, and sharp jets of air startled, even when expected. Beyond the initial challenges, an entire large room was filled with— well, fun things!

The door at the far side of a partially darkened side room was tricky to reach because the floor was slanted, although pictures on the wall appeared as horizontal as the floor outside. Elsewhere a gigantic open–ended wooden barrel lay on its side and turned at a good clip right in line with a walkway. True adventurers dared not bypass this obstacle, for that would risk loss of face! Anyhow, it could be conquered forthrightly by walking slightly sideways and uphill.

Other delights included a long slide whose curves and minor peak could be negotiated most quickly when we riders sat on burlap bags and kept our shoes from dragging. The high slide wore down any resolve to resist departure, for fatigue from climbing its stairway preceded our parents' persuading us to leave the special house of play. As it happens, a further lure to abandon the slide was clearly audible if not visible, for assorted child–made noises echoed now and again from a wall of mirrors waiting to confront oncomers rounding a nearby corner.

The several side–by–side mirrors were large and made of shiny metal, generally smudged by small handprints. The major mystery lay in the awful truth that their curved shapes distorted the images of all who approached, the fair and not so fair alike. No great temptation there to stretch our mouths into hideous grins or to comment about the appearance of others, for the optical tricks were unrelenting to all who stood before them.

As projected images of myself had disappeared when I walked clear of the mirrors' scrutiny decades ago, today's mental images now passed too, though they would return before my hike ended. Meanwhile, a shift in thought occurred as I moved from a paved section of roadway to one surfaced with loose gravel and ruts. In the shift, I recalled a specific destination held in mind for the day, a variant from my more usual impulse–guided sauntering. Early that morning, I resolved to have another look at the frame of a large tepee which stood near the creek bed at the western end of the Abbey land. I would head there, free of angular side trips to explore what caught my fancy along the way.

Not so, it turned out! I was repeatedly drawn aside by many and varied attractions. A glance toward the mountain snow reminded me that my that my early life in four–season settings still urges me to seek seasonal changes throughout the year, and that is possible in the high desert setting. Thereupon I leaped into the future to wonder about when I would be here again.

Several clumps of bunchgrass exposed an unkept resolve to learn why these types of grass grow in bundles and do not spread uniformly over the ground. Scores of unused smudge-pots from the days of orchard–tending pointed me to a past which I had not experienced.

My wildest wonderment was about the origin of limestone. That mental excursus passed through remembering oyster shells collected in mounds near a former residence, thence to musing on the role that algae play in assisting soft living oysters to form their hard protective shells, and finally to question whether tiny algae took part in forming deposits of limestone, as they had vast underground lakes of petroleum.

So the intended straight–out hike was intervened! I began to feel energized beyond the level of relaxed comfort. Then two sounds broke the chain of intrusions. The first was the swish of sand sliding down a nearby slope, no more earth than could be carried in a garden bucket. But why the sudden instability and movement? No lizard or other creaturely instigator was visible, though a light breeze was moving. Could it be that a 'final' supporting grain of sand was moved by the current of air, and others were freed to fall? I considered that insights and mental images also look for escape from wherever they repose until the host is receptive. For the moment, I made peace with the flood of random thoughts.

The second sound came from a source which a shotgun blast made obvious. I spotted three hunters a couple of hundred yards away, and instantly felt a number of concerns.

I wanted to insure that they were aware of my presence, and opined in silent judgment that they were hunting in a posted bird sanctuary—and for quail related to one who had befriended me years before! I was now on guard, but determined to continue my planned hike. Like walking bravely through the Fun House barrel, I would keep face! I yielded to that prompting, turning often to remain aware of the hunters' shifting location and hoping that they were doing likewise for me.

The water–pump shed marked the end of the roadway. I walked on towards a deep cut in the land, remembering that movement of a single grain of sand might have started the tiny avalanche I had heard and seen a few minutes earlier. Prudently standing back from the edge, I could see the creek flowing freely. In former times it had been surely constricted by the soil; now the cut was about thirty feet deep and perhaps two hundred feet wide to accommodate today's tiny stream.

Straight across the gulch was a ranch residence, dominated by household and other objects that had been dumped there over the years. Once again my focus on natural objects was diverted to this sad legacy of frontier mentality— so my judgmental thoughts reacted.

But I also spotted the framework of long poles shaping the uncovered tepee which had launched the day's walk— and a rock–surfaced roadway which I had failed to see in former visits near this site. I made my first visit to this adult version of a house which someone had probably constructed just for fun, and entered to remain silent for several minutes within the skeletal pyramid.

My return walk to the retreat house was filled with a variety of sights and sounds which seemed to insist that I make brief written reminders of their presence. Exhilaration and overload dwelt within me simultaneously. Once again sharp sounds broke into the mixture: a double shotgun blast from a gun pointed upward toward a hovering hawk, but mercifully distant for the bird and myself. For a second time, my reverie was mixed with near–manic imagining, the adrenaline–releasing intrusion repaid by my silent judgment of others present!

There have been other days when my intended meditative sauntering has been overfilled with distractions that were alluring at the time. While writing in my journal shortly after this day's incidents, I realized that what was so animating during the walk seemed flat as I attempted to memorialize it on paper. Other such occasions have been accompanied by a feeling of letdown too, but from the aggregate I have learned about myself. I can affirm that lessons come from high moments, not just from those which are distressful. William James noted in several ways that life is qualified by a change of pace: "Like a bird's life, it seems to be made up of an alternation of flights and perchings."

Exciting moments do not have to be enshrined in writing or otherwise. Important insights will return from wherever they came the first time, and need not be clutched. Fun House experiences enjoyed most fully make real the sacrament of the present moment.

The morning had been characterized by differences which broke into what had begun as a planned hike: variety, sight, sound, plans, intrusions, anxious concern, distant memories, judgments, adrenaline, and much more. Altogether those elements imparted a 'high' feeling. I now remind myself of a need to integrate what comes to me as separate or differentiated, and that takes place in less obvious ways. But such personal appropriation is basic to my ongoing spiritual formation and often calls for intentional support. Otherwise, I shall have a distorted view of life.

A reflective life needs a faithful reflecting mirror. Not so with those in the Fun House! I cannot say how their rippled surfaces would be termed by an optical expert. However, the corner of a medicine chest at home holds a small round concave mirror which I can examine. Like its Fun House relatives, it plays tricks. When I bring my eye close it enlarges. When I back off, reflections first become unfocused; but when I back off still farther, a held object is seen large but inverted. The images can be real or virtual, erect or inverted, enlarged or reduced—depending on where an object and my eye are relative to the mirror surface. My meditative musing, another kind of reflection, imparts outcomes which depend on how I face up to or distance myself from real life experiences providing so much unedited data about my true self.

What a coincidence it is that the words 'concave' and 'retreat' are related, both alluding to a withdrawal from flatness. A concave surface is bowl–shaped, or at least recessed. A concave mirror, like the more familiar convex lens from a scout's pack, can be used to focus sunlight sharply enough to kindle a fire. To be on retreat allows an introcurving personal focus so that important enlightenment is not lost. I can focus or make larger and indistinct, or even inverted, depending on how I choose my distance from usual routines—another insight from a very high day in the high desert.

20
carrying
a desert spirit
home

I have never basked in a summer cruise romance, having never taken a summer cruise! But I recall several camp and retreat experiences that I wanted not to end. Couldn't we have a reunion near home several months from now? Let's do it!

Enthusiastic promises for a get–together seemed for a brief moment a way both to relieve the sadness and to carry high experiences home, somehow insuring their continuity. But the truth is that the great times were not created solely by we participants. The physical settings also contributed greatly. Should we try to reconvene here, in this place which has come to mean so much to us? That's difficult for some of us, is it? Well, maybe we'll see each other next year... a few of us, anyhow. (That way we can see that the place hasn't changed drastically, but will remain as wonderful as it now is!)

Treasuring past visits to St. Andrew's Abbey, I want to protect it as a special place. I incline thus especially after observing extensive home construction taking place some ten miles away in the city of Palmdale. Several years ago I was amused by developers' extravagant naming of housing subdivisions to suggest great forests, rushing streams, seaside resorts, and unbounded space—each of these to describe residences side by side on desert land. Now the rapid spread raises concerns; I am shy after bidding farewell to natural beauty in other regions of America amidst the population growth.

Because the monastic place is special for me, I see the building surge as future encroachment. Obviously thousands of new residents disagree with my assessment; indeed their moving into Antelope Valley probably feels like liberation. My concern for the future reluctantly yields to their present choices. The seesaw feelings urge me to give more care to nature's gifts still there to be received. I realize that I am not inclined to live only for today, stimulated by physical pleasure; but to deny the present would refuse enjoyment of creation which surrounds me. In this monastic setting, I recall that for centuries Benedictine monks have sought a middle course between forgoing nature's bountiful gifts and exploiting them. Periodic stock–taking and gratefulness help me to review the matter beyond elements of real estate, and to push aside the 'black or white' mode of judgment.

I savor my encounters with the gentle side of nature— "The vividness of the here, the spontaneity of the now," Anne Morrow Lindbergh has written. I can rejoice in what is offered, neither needing to explore far afield from the immediate, nor being constrained from continued searching. I need not add gophers or coyotes to my inquiry, though they may come to intrigue me in the future!

Sauntering has taught me to enjoy the journey, not simply to strive to attain goals, whether on life's long trail or on a short morning hike. I discover much that is truly sacred about each present moment, and I respond by freeing up future time intentionally to reflect on that profound reality.

I speculate about the appearance of a 'typical' present-day monk's cell, if there is such a thing. More actively, I have paced cloister paths framing the green central areas of perhaps a dozen ancient abbeys now in ruins. Private cells where solitude was observed, and open cloisters for community work at looms or desks or work tables, each different but equally important, and honored accordingly.

I am impressed by a number of doublets which at first seem poles apart, but are in fact mutually supportive: serene locations and busy activities, solitude and community, worship and work, prayer and service, outreach and inreach, sauntering and insights, action and reflection, a place to live and another to reveal the value of place as a reality. In these pairs I fancy rhythms as basic as those which maintain heartbeat or breathing or nutrition or procreation. What lives in harmony with its opposite bears surprising fruit! In a human life, balance in having and sharing create a sense of fulfillment. I suspect that these mutually supportive life signs are as basic as the throbbing resonance within an atom, or the heart of the Creator!

Out of this musing, I realize that my life does not go around in circles like two airplanes I spotted circling overhead—too narrowly observed, it turned out. I was lying in a thick carpet of grass below the ranch house, idly gazing upward and imagining various scenes in the leaves and shadows of a tree, much as I have done in areas more blessed with fluffy clouds. The aircraft moved in an unleafed opening of bright blue. At first I thought they were awfully close. Several minutes later, the same carelessness! At their third pass I realized that the nearness was intentional: a towplane lifting a sailplane above the desert floor, then releasing the wide–winged one to soar in a lively thermal updraft.

Envy nudged aside, I knew that the pilot of the sailplane could not move just anywhere, not for long at least! The light craft was borne aloft by a column of heated air flowing upward. Turn away from the upflow and the support would not be there. I perceived the need for the pilot's awareness of two centers: the location of the plane and the boundaries of the air column. So it is in my life, I admitted: not simply the two special places of home and retreat but other elements as fundamental as my being and God, who not only created but who continues to nourish me.

By admitting God's presence into the center of my life, my course can be more varied than the near–circular flight of the sailplane. My way becomes more like an ellipse, with two centers: God and myself. Sometimes these centers are far apart, and I can venture widely beyond my assertive individual focus. Later I am drawn back to God when my internal resources wane. With that renewal and assurance, I can chance wonderful adventures of a quite different sort—spiritual, or whatever term applies. And there arc brief moments when the two centers seem identical, when I experience an awesome attunement or unity with the divine.

The invitation to a particular place of retreat remains, even as I travel to other favored spots. Curiously, I find that I know the place better and better as I return from other settings: one time after visiting family on a small island in the Caribbean, and another after traveling to the verdant Piedmont area of Virginia. Some occasions are sad, some joyful, some times are marked by little energy, others by abundant power. Though I may return to the Abbey in various states, the homecoming is to one place, not everywhere. Indeed, I become newly aware that I am not called to be everybody, but only an authentic me. Having several times felt God's presence in one favored place, I come to expect God's presence elsewhere. Among other thoughts, I see this as validating the central Christian doctrine of Incarnation: the spiritual mediated through the material.

The place—any place—is not merely a scene of experience but a primary component of existence. Of course, I have to live somewhere! I see the wisdom of Thoreau's comment about the Saunterer (the one *sans terre*): not one without land or home, but one who is equally at home anywhere. That is a blessing I gratefully accept. I take it to mean that I shall be at home anywhere in the universe—wherever I let my heart be touched and enter into a gentle relationship with what is immediately before me—whether in space or time!

footnotes

page 3
Donald C. Peattie
A Natural History of Western Trees
Boston, Houghton & Mifflin, 1953

p.6
Peggy Larson with Lane Larson
The Deserts of the Southwest
San Francisco, Sierra Club Books, 1927

p.17
Miklos D. F. Udvardy
Audubon Society Field Guide to North American Birds, Western Region
New York, Knopf, 1977

p.22
Henry David Thoreau
On Walking, in *Harvard Classics*
New York, P. F. Collier & Son, 1910

p.26
A. M. Allchin
'Commentaries of Heaven' in *Fairacres Chronicle*
Spring 1990

p.72
John H. Bland
Forests of Lilliput: The Realm of Mosses and Lichens
Englewood Cliffs, Prentice–Hall Inc., 1971

p.75
Thomas Berry
'Saving the Earth,' in *Fellowship in Prayer*

p.85
Henri Nouwen
The Way of the Heart
New York, Ballantine, 1985